PRAISE FOR

I'm The One Who Got Away

"I was enthralled. Andrea Jarrell is a stunning writer, moving deftly through decades in near-cinematic prose (seriously: somebody make this book into a movie!). We're with her in LA, imagining her largely absent father; in Austin, knowing she took a wrong turn; in Maine and D.C. realizing how our childhoods tangle with our grown-up selves. I'm thinking about how imagination is as much a part of memoir as lived experience. I'm thinking about what it means to live in curiosity, not judgment. I'm thinking that I need to stop what I'm doing and read this book again. Like, *immediately.*"
—Megan Stielstra, *The Wrong Way to Save Your Life* and
Once I Was Cool

"Andrea Jarrell's beautiful memoir—her adventurous yet protective single mother; insinuating father/stranger; friends and encounters, lovers and spouse, templates of what she must move beyond, accept, or embrace to become bravely herself—is as riveting as a mystery and as filling as a feast."
—William O'Sullivan, *Washingtonian* magazine

"Andrea Jarrell lets us join her as she gets away, lets us feel the thrilling trajectory of escape as she breaks through familial and personal patterns into a freer, more joyful life. This honest, thoughtful memoir is written with great compassion; Jarrell's love for her family, and for her own journey as a woman, rises off the page, even in the most painful moments. She reminds us to be our own liberators, our own witnesses, to appreciate the majesty of our own everyday world."
—Gayle Brandeis, *The Art of Misdiagnosis: A Memoir* and
The Book of Dead Birds

"Beautifully told with great wisdom and clear-eyed courage, Andrea Jarrell has mapped her personal journey in life—the fears and obstacles and losses as well as the joys and comforts of love and finding her own sense of home. I could not put it down."

—Jill McCorkle, *Life After Life* and *Going Away Shoes*

"Haunted by her father's absence and riveted by her single mother's cautionary tales, Andrea Jarrell longed for the 'stuff of ordinary families' even as she was drawn to the drama of her parents' larger-than-life love. In her wise and resonant memoir, Jarrell revisits stories starring wolves in cowboy clothing and lambs led astray by charming savior-saboteurs, to lovingly recount how she escaped a narrative she'd learned by heart and wrote her own version of a happy life."

—Elizabeth Mosier, *The Playgroup* and *My Life as a Girl*

"A charming snake of a B-movie actor father who'll steal your heart and leave you the bruises of abuse. A smart, determined mother forging a life for her and her daughter while looking over her shoulder for fear—and sometimes in the hope—he'll track them down. In a lesser writer's hands, this story might be rendered as Technicolor melodrama and in glaring neon prose. But Andrea Jarrell is conducting a far more meaningful investigation into the choices life has presented her, the mistakes she has repeated, and the vivid resolve to emerge into the life she's greatly earned. It's her candor and her courage and the memoir's clean, sure, unflinching voice that we come away remembering."

—Douglas Bauer, author of *What Happens Next?: Matters of Life and Death*

I'm
the
one
who
got
away

I'm
the
one
who
got
away

a memoir

By

ANDREA JARRELL

[swp]

SHE WRITES PRESS

Published 2017
Printed in the United States of America
ISBN: 978-1-63152-260-4 pbk
ISBN: 978-1-63152-261-1 ebk
Library of Congress Control Number: 2017936163

Book design by Stacey Aaronson

For information, address:
She Writes Press
1563 Solano Ave #546
Berkeley, CA 94707

She Writes Press is a division of SparkPoint Studio, LLC.

For my forever love, Brad

For my precious children, Carson and Daniel

And for my beloved mother—my original hero

Part I

SUSANNAH WAS MURDERED JUST BEFORE CHRISTMAS but I didn't find out until after New Year's. When my cell phone rang, we were making the long trek between Michigan and Maine after spending the holidays with my in-laws. My husband, Brad, was at the wheel, kids strapped into their car seats munching a snack, my feet propped on the dash. As barren treetops flitted by, messy tangles of birds' nests catching my eye, the voice on the other end of the line told me she was killed in the house across the street from ours—a large cedar-shingled two-story with a barn in back.

The houses in our neighborhood stood far apart. From the front step of our blue Cape at the top of a mile-long driveway, I could just make out the cedar roof beyond a small pond on our property and a thick line of fir trees across the road. Even if we'd been home, I couldn't have prevented her murder. I know that. Brad and I probably wouldn't even have heard the gunshots. We might have been sitting in our living room watching television or upstairs reading bedtime stories to our son and daughter.

When it happened, the co-op preschool that Susannah's

son and my children attended was already on holiday break. The day the break began, Brad and I had loaded up our SUV, bundled the kids into the car, and headed to Michigan. In those days, before Facebook and Twitter, we'd remained blissfully cocooned from the rest of the world.

I didn't understand at first why I sobbed at the news of Susannah's death. There was the violence of it, the throat-choking sadness for her little boy, and the wrongness of anyone robbed of life, much less someone so young. But there was more to it than that. Especially when I admitted to myself that I'd always been uneasy around Susannah, never wanting to get too close to her.

Eventually, all the cues from my memories about why her murder hit me so hard began to glimmer like flagstones on a moonlit path. A path that paved the way, inevitably, back to my mother. As I connected those dots, my sorrow over Susannah's death revealed what I was only beginning to realize—how desperate I was to escape my mother's choices and the life I feared I was destined to live.

∞

Brad and I had been living in Maine for a few years when Susannah was killed. We were in our early thirties, just starting out in our marriage and our lives as parents. Before Maine, we'd always been city people. Our move from Los Angeles to the idyllic, seaport town of Camden was the first of what we expected would be many adventures in our life together.

Camden is the childhood home of Edna St. Vincent Millay, the town where the movie *Peyton Place* was filmed, and, rumor has it, a haven for retired CIA spies. Locals looking to move know to put their houses on the market during the summer, when tourists fall in love with the quaintness of it all: the harbor, the lupine-covered hills, the centuries-old stone walls, the Oreo black-and-white cows. But Maine winters are for a hardy few, and the smart looky-loos come to their senses before any money changes hands.

We moved to Camden knowing what we were getting into. Brad had been offered a two-year gig at the Institute for Global Ethics to work on a project about running positive political campaigns. I saw the move as a way to leave my workaday life as the public relations director of a small college—to trade in my pantyhose and suits for jeans and sweaters and to get back to writing. Fully expecting to return to L.A. in a couple of years, we found tenants for our small house there. But two years turned into two more, and five years after moving we finally unloaded our Spanish-style fixer-upper in L.A., unsure if we would ever head west again.

Moving to Camden felt a little like we'd entered the witness protection program—so far from everyone we'd known, plunked down into a new life. I took to that life more easily than one might expect, embracing it with "pinch me" elation: pancakes on Sundays, a fully stocked pantry with an extra freezer for meat, trips to the pumpkin patch, red wagons in the driveway, rain boots and slickers, mittens and parkas. This was the stuff of ordinary families, which I'd carefully observed during childhood sleep-overs. Having grown up in a series of small apartments with my single mother, who was much more interested in books and travel than picket fences and seasonal door wreaths, I kept waiting for the residents of Camden to discover that I didn't belong.

Oh, I knew how to look the part at Mommy and Me music classes, or when it was my turn to handle a baking project at the preschool, or while hanging out under a wide-brimmed straw hat at the local beach, my kids appropriately slathered with sunscreen and playing with sand pails and shovels. But I still felt inferior, the way I had as a kid when I would tell friends and their parents that my mother was a lawyer rather than a legal secretary. I told that lie right up through college, even though the thought of being found out made me queasy.

Being around certain people prompted such lies in me—in Camden, people like Kim Tate and her husband, Jack. Kim was a tall, athletic blonde who'd gone to Yale. She'd met Jack—also tall, but dark and handsome enough—on the train between New Haven and New York City one afternoon when they were both in college. With their good looks and money, the Tates were small-town famous. Other mothers at our preschool had a crush on Jack; one of them went so far as to tell Kim that she looked forward to receiving their photo Christmas card so she could moon over him. I had more of a crush on Kim, whose three perfect little children were spaced a year and a half apart, lined up like cherub-faced Russian nesting dolls in hand-knitted sweaters she'd designed and made.

Our oldest kids—Kim's and mine—were in the fours and

fives class at the co-op preschool along with Susannah's son. If Kim was on the elite end of the social spectrum, Susannah was on the other. Or at least that's where, I admit now, I put her. Almost from the moment I met her, something about Susannah made me steer clear. If I saw her faded, rust-colored Toyota in the school's parking lot, I stayed in my own car, behind darkened windows. I waited to go inside until after she and her son emerged from the school, their fingers laced, the day's artwork flapping in Susannah's other hand.

She was one of those pretty girl-women—twenty-one, twenty-three, twenty-five? If she hadn't been a mother, she might have seemed even younger, like a teenager with her whole life ahead of her. I'd seen fathers at the preschool watching her, trying to be nonchalant as they homed in on her. You could tell that she'd grown up attracting such attention and was no longer surprised or moved by it. At first, I wondered if my impulse to avoid her was simple jealousy because she was younger and sexier than I was. Her short skirts and angled beret over long corn-silk hair displayed a confidence that I'd never had.

Later, I noticed that she avoided me and the other parents as well, never lingering to chat on the playground. She always smiled but hurried purposefully—my mother had projected a similar defensive smile when she attended my school events or collected me from a sleepover. *Just we two*, my mother always used to say. As I watched Susannah, I could feel how tightly her hand grasped her son's as they exited the preschool, holding on to each other and their place in the world. Only after her death did it dawn on me that Susannah's confidence, like my mother's, was designed to let other parents know she was doing fine, even though we outnumbered her two to one.

The only time I remember talking to Susannah was when she and her son came to my daughter's birthday party. I hadn't really wanted to invite them, but my mother taught me to be kind even when it is insincere. It was July; all the preschool parents stood around on our wide green lawn as kids took turns barreling down a giant yellow Slip 'N Slide.

I happened to be standing next to Susannah when my daughter began opening gifts. The present Susannah's son brought was a wooden fairy wand that his mother had painted dark blue and topped with a glitter-encrusted star. Susannah had written my daughter's name in silver along the handle. We watched as the birthday girl opened the gift and ran her small hand along the letters of her name. Susannah leaned sideways to me, our shoulders touching, and said, "I knew she would like it. She's such an artist."

I imagined them together in the co-op preschool on one of Susannah's volunteer days. I could see her asking my daughter about the painting she was working on. Susannah would've bent down to eye level, pushing her long blonde hair behind one shoulder as she did.

Some time after that, as I pulled into the preschool lot, I noticed a man sitting in the passenger seat of Susannah's car. I was surprised to recognize him. He was the fit, tanned man who lived in the house across the road from ours, where he operated a moving, refuse, and antiques business out of his adjacent barn. His name was Craig. When we first arrived from California, Brad had hired him to help move us in. Admiring Craig's Yankee entrepreneurism, my husband marveled, "He's got it covered. He'll move it, dump it, or sell it."

I remember being inexplicably happy to see my neighbor in Susannah's car, happier still when I passed her familiar Toyota parked in front of his house. It intrigued me to think of how they might have met. Perhaps he had hired her to answer the phones for his business. Or they'd struck up a conversation in Cappy's bar on Main Street. There was no question of why Susannah would appeal to him. But I could also see why he would appeal to her. In his late forties, he was attractive in a town where single men were few and far between. She might have said to herself, *Try older, try wiser.* He would be a good provider, a role model for her little boy. I pictured them together—sheets rumpled, his tanned workman's hands on her milky skin. I imagined him thanking his lucky stars each day to have such a lovely girl on his arm.

I'd once imagined such meetings for my mother: a new client or lawyer in her firm who would appear one day and change our lives. I wondered what Susannah's secret was. How had she managed to find a partner and step into a new, safer life when my mother had not?

∼

Like a bedtime story, my mother used to tell me of our escape from my father. She'd light a cigarette, press it to her elegant lips, exhale, and begin. Benign stories at first. But even in those early, seemingly innocent stories, there was a streak of violence. Singeing her eyelashes and eyebrows trying to light the stove in their first apartment. My father's compound fracture from an arm-wrestling match with a buddy on his birthday—the humerus splitting right through the camel hair jacket my mother had given him. "His muscles were stronger than bone," she'd said with a trace of awe. As I got older, I would hear how his jealousy made him suspicious and mean. Drinking made his rages worse. She told people she was clumsy to explain her bruised skin and black eyes.

The day my mother first felt me move inside her, she began plotting to leave my father. Like Susannah, my mother had been a girl-woman—just nineteen years old. She'd grown scared of what this man who slept beside her with a gun under his pillow might do to us one day when my crying got too much for him, or when yet another man admired her beauty. Somehow I'd given her the courage to escape.

Our getaway car had been a teal blue Corvair. I was just a year old. From then on, she'd literally and figuratively strapped me in beside her—her precious cargo.

∽

My neighbor Craig was a mild man, nothing like my father. And yet he'd acted on the same jealousy and possessiveness that my mother had run away from. When Susannah told Craig it was over, was it her little boy she was thinking of?

It was Kim Tate who telephoned me as we were driving home from Michigan. After she told me what had happened to Susannah, she kept saying "I'm so sorry," when she heard me crying. "I didn't know you two were close."

Of course, we hadn't been close at all, but I immediately thought of the last time I'd seen her car in Craig's driveway. The sense of relief I'd had, thinking she'd found her happy ending. Thinking she could loosen the grip on her small son's hand just a little because they were safe at last.

He'd shot her twice, using an antique pistol from his shop. According to the papers, after he killed her, he called his grown son and left the voicemail message: "I've done something stupid." Then he hung up and killed himself.

It wasn't hard to imagine Craig's desperate pleading as he'd tried to make Susannah stay. I could picture him grabbing her arm. She would have tried to shake him off, her blonde hair flying as she tossed the few things she'd brought to his house into an overnight bag. When he left the room, she would not have known that he'd gone to the barn to look for a gun.

Passing our pond—frozen and covered in snow—I heard the engine labor as our car climbed the long driveway, our blue house coming into view. As we pulled into the garage, firewood neatly stacked and dry by the mudroom door, how I wished I could run to Susannah now, wrap my arms around her and tell her to get in that rust-colored Toyota and drive as far away as possible. Save her the way my mother had saved us.

Yet how could I have rescued her when I hadn't even allowed myself to know her?

In my mind's eye, I saw her sitting in my kitchen, drinking coffee with me. I imagined her son playing with my kids on the floor of our living room. But that had never happened.

As cute as her little boy was, I can admit now that I'd written him off as damaged goods. Damaged the way I'd been at his age. Jealous of what my friends had, prone to elaborate lies and petty thefts, hitting and hair pulling when no one was looking.

Eventually, I would understand that it had never been Susannah's youth or prettiness that kept me away from her. It was her aloneness. That old, familiar, *just-we-two* aloneness I couldn't bear to see up close again. As if somehow it might turn its eye on me and suck me back in—snatch away this life I'd ached for—my husband, my children, and the pancakes on Sundays. Despite having Brad and the kids, a part of me feared that the only place I would ever really belong was with my mother. Just we two against the world.

Five
Flashes
of
Teeth

1
—

LIKE A CATHOLIC PRIEST WITH A DIRECT LINE TO GOD, for many years my mother was my only conduit to my father—the interpreter of his handsomeness, his viciousness, his cockiness. We'll call him Nick, though that is not his real name. When they met, Nick never told my mother he wanted to be famous. Perhaps back then he didn't even know it himself. But his need to be loved—as clichéd as that sounds—all but preordained it. And nature was on his side. Indeed, I once read in a movie magazine that for a male star to be truly handsome he needed four things: a large head, good teeth, a deep philtrum (those two lines between your nose and lips), and a cleft chin. My father had them all.

The first time I saw him on television, I was seven. My mother and I were living in a little apartment near UCLA. During a commercial on *Marcus Welby, M.D.*, she whispered, "It's Nick."

She said his name with a *Did you see that?* incredulity, as if a coyote had just crept out of one of the nearby canyons and flitted by our window. A coyote—or maybe a wolf.

I had less than thirty seconds to study the man catching a blonde's Ultra Brite kiss. But for years after that toothpaste commercial, I kept an eye out for my father's cleft chin and brown eyes. I would say to my mother, "Is that him?" pointing at the television. I could never be sure. I had to rely on her to lean in close, her head next to mine to direct my line of sight as if to say, *There, look, there he is.* And sure enough, then I could see him. He was the corrupt businessman on *Charlie's Angels*, the detective who got shot on a two-part *Police Woman*, the city politician on *The Rockford Files*.

2
—

Once, when my mother read an essay I'd written, she asked, "How did you know our Impala was burgundy?" I didn't know how to answer. Did she tell me, or did I just guess because of course burgundy would have been the color they chose? I'd heard some of the details of their life together, turning them over in my child's mind when my mother and her friends smoked and sipped from pink cans of Tab and talked about men and failed marriages and self-improvement. On those occasions, I would stay very still so the women would forget I was there, playing beside the couch, listening. For years, my parents' movie played on the screen of my mind: the car pulling up, my father—her co-star—behind the wheel.

Nick dropped out of college around the same time his family relocated from Texas to my mother's small Colorado town. She was sixteen. He was twenty, all swagger and audacity—the older brother of the new kid at her high school. Nick was the firstborn in a family of five, the black sheep and golden boy in one. After losing his University of Arizona football scholarship because of an injury, he moved into his parents' new house, commandeering the best bedroom for himself. He spent his days ordering his brothers around, eating his mother's home cooking, and considering his next move. As it turned out, his next move was my mother.

Despite the college scholarships she'd already lined up— she wanted to be a photojournalist or a graphic artist—she accepted the tiny diamond engagement ring he gave her for Christmas. "He was the most exciting person I'd ever met," she has told me. "Man, woman, child, or beast—it didn't matter—he could make you his."

My mother suspects her parents consented to the marriage mostly because they were afraid she was pregnant. She wasn't, and to prove it she asked her mother to take in the waists of all her skirts and dresses, reassuring her parents and silencing the school gossips. On a January morning a few months before her seventeenth birthday, she walked down the aisle with Nick.

Mere weeks after the wedding, he took her away from her friends and family. The newlyweds left Colorado, moving first to Texas, where she knew no one and he knew everyone, and then to Las Vegas. Nick got a job selling advertising for the *Las Vegas Sun*. With his winning smile, he could sell anything.

In a town chockablock with fame, my father began to

taste the possibility of his own. As successful as he was, he'd never seen himself as a nine-to-fiver. Feeling he was destined for bigger things, he learned quickly how to sidle up to Frank Sinatra's big table and get invited to sit down. He had a talent for schmoozing with Sammy Davis Jr. and Dean Martin. Soon his best buddy was Lindsay Crosby, Bing's son.

Even today, years after I first heard the story of my parents' meeting, I feel a pull in my gut—a place right at the top of my ribcage—a *what if* tug of regret for my mother. What if she hadn't met him by those bleachers that day at Montezuma-Cortez High School, home of the Panthers. What if?

As a kid, hearing her story, knowing what came after, I always wanted to scream at her the way you do when a character in a horror film starts down the stairs into a dark basement.

But my mother's teenage self never heard my warnings. Growing up, I asked her many times why she went with him so willingly and why her parents let her go. The answers I got—"Things were different then. People got married younger"— never satisfied me. I understood that "wife" rather than "photojournalist" must have sounded like the safer choice in 1959. But I expected someone as smart as my mother to be, well, smarter. I wanted my mother's teenage self to see the writing on the wall. More than anything, I wanted her to resist my father's charms.

3

The night Nick turned twenty-two, his childhood friend TJ brought several buddies and their wives and girlfriends from

Texas to Vegas to celebrate. Arriving at the Sands Hotel, the men wore white dinner jackets, while my mother and the other women wore silk and organza dresses. They headed to a reserved table near the dance floor as Nick worked the room, smiling and waving.

Still, he kept an eye on my mother. He always knew exactly where she was. He looked over at the precise moment one of TJ's friends moved to pull out her chair for her. My mother didn't want the guy to hold her chair. She knew better.

In seconds, Nick was by her side. "Hey, partner," he said to the interloper. They stood side by side behind my mother's chair. Nick put a hand on the guy's back. "Thanks so much for keeping an eye out for her." He said it smoothly, so there was no gauging his mood.

"Don't mention it," TJ's friend said.

"I should be shot, huh? Leaving a beauty like this all alone." Nick laughed.

My mother said, "Let's all sit down, why don't we?"

Nick gave her that pursed-lip smile of his, but his eyes were hard and he was thinking.

"She *is* a beauty, too. Don't you think?" He traced one finger along her bare shoulder.

My mother willed TJ's friend, who was still standing there, not to say anything, not to take the bait. But he did. Turning to face my father, he smiled and said, "You don't want to leave her alone too long."

The smile is what set Nick off. He jabbed his finger into the guy's chest so hard his shoulder jerked back. TJ stood up.

"Nick, come on." But my father never listened to TJ when they were kids. Why would he now?

"You looking to get it wet?" he said, jabbing his finger again.

"Whoa, buddy. I didn't mean anything by it."

"Oh, now I'm your buddy? Seems more like you want to be my wife's buddy."

The bouncers at the door were watching now.

"Let's just sit," my mother said as the three of them stood in a little cluster around her chair.

"You want to sit with this limp dick? You thinking about that?"

"Please," she said. "Everyone's looking."

"Is that what you care about?" My father smiled, a glimmer of white teeth between his lips. Then he raised his arms as if he was feeling rain from the sky. He turned in a full circle and bowed, relishing making a scene. He pressed closer to my mother. She could feel his pant leg rub against her stockings, his breath in her ear. "I thought it was this limp dick you cared about."

Taking a step back, he shoved her chair into the backs of her knees so she lost her balance and sat down hard. Then he took his seat beside her. The band began to play. Couples moved to the dance floor. My mother did not meet the eyes of the others at the table, and they knew better than to look her way. Nick draped his arm around her shoulder. She could feel him keeping time to the music, one foot tapping.

4
—

Beyond beauty and intelligence, even at sixteen my mother had an Olympian's dedication to hard work. Employers spotted this right away. The Nevada Club, an upscale casino, hired her as an assistant bookkeeper. When she first started working at the club, she didn't know anything about gambling. From the casino's reports, she learned how the games worked—chuck-a-luck, 21, and Baccarat.

The Nevada Club catered to a better class of customer than many of the casinos, but the alley running between the club's office and the casino was a dumping ground for mob hits. After police found one too many bodies there, the casino posted guards in the alley. Those guards escorted my mother and the other secretaries as they carried check signature plates and money across the alley to the casino's safe. These guards would look the other way when my mother lingered in the casino to play a few rounds of blackjack. Even though she was underage, the dealers didn't question her. Maybe they knew a pretty woman would attract more players to the table. Or maybe they detected the black eyes she covered with makeup and took pity on her.

Either way, in the end it would be my mother's industriousness and talent for gambling—along with my father's lust for fame—that allowed her to escape.

One of the ways Nick held a tight rein on his wife was to keep her isolated from her family and friends. They'd been married for almost three years when I was born. During those years, he'd allowed her to see her parents only a handful of times. But just before my first birthday, he relaxed his rule.

My father had a plan to save rent money for the summer by sending my mother and me to live with her parents while he moved in with Lindsay Crosby. My mother went along with his scheme, knowing that as soon as we left, he and Lindsay were headed to Miami to do as they pleased. She knew it wasn't a break from rent he wanted but rather a vacation from married life. Not that marriage had stopped him from doing what he liked anyway. Twice he'd told her to go to the doctor to see if he'd given her gonorrhea.

But now she didn't care, because she had a plan of her own.

By then her parents had left Colorado and moved to Fresno, a city in California's Central Valley. Her blackjack stash had grown. When Nick put us on that little plane, he had no idea that my mother had already shipped several boxes of her things to her parents' house. He had no idea she intended to leave him for good.

My grandparents lived in a brand new house and had a bedroom waiting for us. They'd planted gardenias, my mother's favorite flower, by the front door. During those first few months when she thought we'd really gotten away, safety smelled like those gardenias. In my mother's mind, the flower's perfume was linked to the sound of her key turning in her parents' front door as she arrived home from her new job.

While my grandmother cared for me, my mother and grandfather went off to work. The three of them reunited for dinner each day much like they'd done when my mother was a girl. The motorized garage door would signal my grandfather's arrival home from his trucking business. Before entering the house, he would leave his shoes by the back door. It was the early 1960s and all the men wore hard, lace-up shoes and dark socks of ribbed nylon, ankle or knee length.

In his stocking feet, my grandfather would pad into the living room. Exhausted from rising before dawn to supervise his crew of truckers and mechanics, he'd settle into his leather recliner. Pushing back, his feet rose on the footrest. That's when I, a toddler playing nearby, would start screaming. My grandmother and mother would hurry in from the kitchen where they'd been making dinner. A spatula or tasting spoon still in one hand, one of them would scoop me up, desperate to comfort me, but unable to determine the source of my distress.

At last, they solved the mystery: my grandfather's socks. Back in the apartment Nick and my mother shared in Las Vegas, from my vantage point—a crawling baby on the floor—I must only have seen my father's feet and his dark socks each time he came for her, jealous again, raging again, beating her again.

5
—

All summer, my mother had maintained the fiction that she and I were going back to Vegas in the fall. Nick had been calling her from the road—Miami, Texas, and Mexico, where he and Lindsay were following a matador friend on the bullfighting circuit. But toward the end of August, she finally broke the news that she wasn't coming back.

Suddenly, he was desperate to have her. He began calling her dozens of times a day, screaming, pleading, putting Lindsay on the line to talk "sense" to her. This went on for days until he said: "I'll kill myself. Do you want that on your head?" My grandparents blocked his calls after that.

There was nothing left for Nick to do but get on a plane to Fresno.

When my mother would tell the story of his arrival in California, she'd close her eyes, shivering at the memory of his scent. She'd caught a whiff of Nick's lingering cologne in the elevator of her office building on her way back from lunch. "My instinct is still to throw up from fear," she'd tell me. She'd known he would come for her, which may have made it worse when what she feared actually happened. Stepping out of the elevator, an uneaten tuna sandwich on toast in a little bag by her side, she felt sure that he was waiting for her by her desk. Sweat began to bead along her spine, dampening her bra and dress. I would try to imagine what Canoe cologne smelled like. I would see her pressing the elevator button again, turning around and heading home.

He *had* been there. When she didn't come back to her desk after lunch that day, Nick drove to her parents' house, parking down the block. He watched and waited until my grandparents left. Once my mother was alone, he stood on the grass in the front yard, calling her name. She hid on the floor of her bedroom, huddling over me and trying to keep me quiet. When she didn't answer, he circled the house, jiggling the door handles and windows, searching for a way to get in.

The neighborhood was new and isolated, the houses far apart. "You never knew what he would do," my mother has said. "I kept waiting for him to smash one of the windows."

"I know you're in there," he called. He pressed his face to the sliding glass door, cupping his big hands to create shade, trying to see inside. "Let me in," he said like the Big Bad Wolf. "Let me in."

He yelled and banged on the door for nearly an hour. Finally the police arrived. A neighbor must have called them. They didn't arrest my father, but they told him to move along.

He came back the next day but this time my grandfather was ready. A soldier and a man who'd kept crews of oil workers and truck drivers in line, he confronted my father and threatened to call the police again and have him arrested. Perhaps like an animal that grows bored when its prey climbs high into a tree, or perhaps simply to tally his losses and re-group, Nick retreated. But back in Vegas he continued hounding my mother, vacillating between sending flowers and threatening telegrams. She was in the midst of filing for divorce, anticipating an ugly battle, when her luck turned.

Frank Sinatra was filming a new movie and he had a part for my father. *Lady in Cement* would turn out to be Nick's big break. By the time a sheriff served him with divorce papers, he must have thought he was on the brink of stardom. Why be saddled with alimony and child support? He was a no-show in divorce court. After a judge granted full custody of me to my mother, she made legal arrangements for my grandmother to be my guardian should anything happen to her. But taking no more chances, she loaded up her new Corvair and set about disappearing into the vastness of Los Angeles. She even changed our last name, thinking that surely then he would never find us.

"People always said Nick was good-looking," my mother told me not long ago. "But that's not what I cared about. That wasn't it at all. It was the way he carried himself on those long, bowed legs of his. It was his throaty laugh and flash of white teeth that always got me. It was the way he seemed to know all my secrets—not only that, but he found them amusing." A slight smile crept over her lips when she said this.

Perhaps if I'd understood from the beginning that even after all she'd been through, even after we escaped and began our new life in L.A., she could still be drawn to my father's charms, then perhaps I would have understood that the wolf would always be at our door.

Miracle
Mile

IT WAS LUNCHTIME ON THE MIRACLE MILE—A STRETCH
of Wilshire Boulevard in Los Angeles that's not quite downtown and not quite the West Side. My mother walked beside
me in her crisp linen dress. Beneath the linen, her stockings
and slip made a *fft fft* shifting sound, keeping time to the
click of her slingback pumps. Heat waves bent the air. Pedes-
trians hurried from one air-conditioned building to the next,
emptying the streets. Streets that had civilized what was once
ice, then tar pits, then desert. All had made way for the City
of Angels.

Beside my mother, I was office appropriate in a banana
yellow cotton skirt and top combo. I was eleven and it was
1973, when all the clothes were Laffy Taffy colors.

From elementary school through high school, I spent my
summers working with my mother, who was a secretary in a
lawyer's office. Lunchtime was the highlight of my day. On
that particular day, at my request, we were headed past the
office towers and the gas station on the corner to the lunch
truck for *gorditas*. I anticipated the greasy scent of the truck

and the weight of the silver-wrapped sandwich I would carry back to my mother's office.

The lawyer she worked for was a former FBI Special Agent who had investigated the Black Dahlia murder. The Dahlia was a beautiful, dark-haired young woman famously mutilated and left in a field during the 1940s. My mother and I had watched a made-for-TV-movie about this woman, whose looseness was said to have contributed to her death. Even thirty years later, a woman on her own, divorced like my mother, risked speculation—blame for whatever unhappy ending might befall her.

"They assume you're cheap," my mother would say, wrinkling her nose at the word "cheap." It was one of the worst ways she herself could judge you. Dyed hair, hoop earrings, white shoes, gum chewing, smoking on the street all marked you as loose in my mother's eyes. Even though she was barely thirty, she did not participate in the swinging '70s. My mother wanted always to be above reproach—to prove that she was better than the way she sounded on paper—apartment-dwelling single mother, divorced, no college.

After working at the FBI, the lawyer my mother worked for started practicing probate law. He wrote wills for little old ladies whose pack-rat houses belied their squirreled-away wealth. One of the first office tasks my mother gave me was to go through a small wooden file box filled with thumbed-over index cards and remove all the client cards marked DECEASED. In my mind, "Dahlia" and "deceased" mingled with a macabre thrill.

The lawyer took long vacations—five or six weeks at a

stretch during which he and his wife ate their way across Europe. When he was gone my mother ran the show, which meant the two of us were on our own for most of the summer. Sometimes after working all day, when we got home she would make us Coke floats for dinner. We ate them in our nightgowns playing Scrabble or watching old movies late into the night. During *West Side Story*—one of our favorites—I would dance around our apartment wearing my mother's hand-me-down peignoir singing, "I feel pretty." And in those moments, I believed that my freckles and red hair, which didn't ring the "pretty" bell, would one day add up to my mother's porcelain skin and brunette beauty.

In the morning, we would drag ourselves into the office like hungover roommates. We'd skip breakfast. By lunchtime I was ready to eat.

On the lookout for the *gorditas* truck, I was squinting into the next block when my mother and I were forced to slow our pace. We'd come upon a scene taking up the width of the sidewalk. Three boys about my age, on the brink of becoming teenagers, were walking backward, facing us. In between them and us was a woman trying to get past them. My mother and I followed. Witnesses.

I couldn't see the woman's face, but she seemed old to me. She wore a short floral skirt with a faded tank top, the skin on her arms loose and flabby. Her hair was the color of ashes, dirty in the light of the beating sun. A zip-up sweat-shirt hung over one shoulder, and she scooted along in high heels with no stockings like a little girl playing dress-up.

The boys puckered up at her, making kissing noises. Laughing, they played at something that would be more menacing as they got older. They did not touch her but they moved in front of her, blocking her way. She tried to get around them. Once. Twice. Three times. Then I heard her low whine as it boiled to a growl. She jutted her head at them the way a goose honks violently at a predator, and she picked up the hem of her skirt—delicately as if to curtsy.

As the woman lifted her skirt waist-high, I saw that she wasn't wearing any underwear. My mother pulled me into the street to hurry by. The woman's tormentors froze, and the shock on one boy's face caught my eye as I passed. Turning back, I took in what he saw—the woman's dark pubic hair beneath her raised skirt, a grown-up eyeful he was not ready for. The woman dropped her hem and moved past them, free at last.

Once we were some distance away, I whispered, "Why did she *do* that?" With my newly forming breasts and hips, my impulse was to protect myself. Especially the part of me that felt vulnerable to boys and men. But this woman had done the opposite.

"She's not well, baby," my mother said, eyeing me. I looked over my shoulder and saw the woman cutting through the gas station, moving on her way. With the lift of her skirt, she'd called their bluff, stopped them in their tracks. She might have been unwell—disturbed—but even then I knew I'd witnessed something powerful.

A few years later, when I was a teenager, my mother and I were exiting a Metro car in Paris. By then, my fully developed body always seemed to announce its presence in a way that I wasn't ready for. As we left the car, pressing into the crowd, a man behind me cupped his hand between my legs. Shamed by his grab, my cheeks red, afterward, I told my mother what had happened. She berated herself.

"I should've made you wear a slip," she said, glancing at the scoops and curves of my light cotton dress. To my mother, a slip—that thin membrane between proper and cheap—could make a difference in how men treated you. A slip might save you from ending up in a field like the Black Dahlia.

I had yet to begin challenging my mother's view of the world. But even then I wondered: What if what really saved you was the courage to growl, to honk, to lift your skirt?

Traveling
Companions

MY MOTHER AND I WERE ON THE SLOW LOCAL TRAIN bound for Rome. I was fifteen. We had started our journey in Venice. Now the train was stopped in Florence, waiting for new passengers to board.

We were alone in a compartment of six seats, three on each side facing the middle. We'd chosen to sit opposite one another by the window. When the compartment's wooden door slid open, we looked up from our books. A small man with a bald, age-spotted head stood in the doorway. He ran his hand over his head—a habit no doubt left over from days when his hair needed smoothing. He made a grand bow to my mother, who lowered her green Michelin guide. She granted him her lovely smile, welcoming him into the compartment like he was a guest arriving at her dinner-party door. Turning to me, he made his bow in miniature. In the movement I saw him think the word *signorina*. Trying a smile, I knew before I began it would not match my mother's.

He stowed his leather bag in the metal rack on my mother's side and chose the seat closest to the door, leaving a space between them. As I watched him settle in, I nicknamed him Danieli, after one of the most deluxe hotels in Venice. He opened his *La Repubblica* across his lap. I noticed his eyes wander past the pages of his newspaper to my mother's legs—her graceful ankle and high calf. He glanced at her breasts, snug in a simple dress of light green wool that matched her eyes, then up to her face and the freshness of her unlined skin. Did he realize this young woman he was clearly appreciating was my mother? People were always shocked to discover it. Not only because of her youth, but also because of her dark hair next to my auburn. Her fair, flawless skin next to my freckles.

I turned to the window, still pouting about being on the wrong train and blaming my mother. We had planned to be on an express that offered a restaurant car complete with white tablecloths and waiters. But that morning, after arriving at the station in Venice, we'd learned the express was sold out. "*No, è pieno,*" the ticket seller had said and then urged us to take the local. My mother explained to me that it was a national holiday so the trains were packed but the slower train was leaving in just a few minutes. We could catch it if we hurried.

This never would have happened on previous trips, when she'd planned out every detail. But she'd said we were "old hands" at this traveling thing now. Excited by the idea that we were going native and leaving more to chance, she'd made no reservations for the fancy train. So we'd been stuck with the local, not even having a moment to buy food at the station before we left.

Perhaps if I hadn't picked a fight with her the night before—if we hadn't gotten up late, spent and groggy from arguing—we would have arrived in time to secure tickets on the fast train. We could have been sitting across from one another enjoying a meal, safe from potential perils.

⌒∾

My mother once told me that she'd heard a radio broadcast about Paris when she was four years old. From then on she yearned to see Europe—a desire her parents and most of her many aunts, uncles, and cousins found peculiar. Europe was a place they'd fought the war to end all wars. Why would anyone go back?

My grandfather's youngest brother was a kindred spirit though. Just six years her senior, Uncle Don and my mother were more like cousins. A gay man in a Southern Baptist family, my uncle had moved from his small-town Oklahoma birthplace to Los Angeles, where he could live an unmarried life without raising eyebrows. He and my mother each longed for culture and became one another's safe "dates." They played tennis at the local high school, took painting classes on Sundays, and dressed up to go to Broadway shows.

But their biggest adventure was a trip to Europe just before my mother's thirtieth birthday. They saved all year and spent the month of August in London, Paris, Rome, and Florence. I stayed in Fresno with my grandparents. I think my grandmother thought the trip would be a one-time, get-it-out-of-your-system experience for my mother. But the opposite was true. On the plane home, all she could think about was coming back the following year and bringing me.

By the time I graduated from high school, we'd been to France, England, Italy, Austria, Holland, and Germany. We'd cruised the Greek islands, roamed the Grand Bazaar in Istanbul, and sailed up the Nile to Luxor, Aswan, and Abu Simbel. Despite all this grand travel, we hadn't struck it rich. We owned no property, had no investments, and did not save for the future except for these trips. But my mother worked hard. She'd gone to night school to become a paralegal and was making a decent salary by then. She managed our apartment building for reduced rent, and she did people's taxes and balanced their books for extra money—all of which went into the travel account. My grandmother continued to ask when my mother was going to stop "traipsing around," marry again, and live in a house with a man who provided for her. For the longest time, I wondered that, too.

Instead, my mother visited the world's romantic spots with me. In Venice, we'd passed beneath the Bridge of Sighs in a gondola. Our handsome gondolier had given me his hand when I stepped onto the unsteady boat. I knew the legend that if you kissed under the bridge your love would last forever, and as he steered us beneath it, I was embarrassed to be sitting on the cushioned seat beside my mother.

"Better to see these things with each other than not at all," she had said more than once. "I'm spoiling you," she teased. "Whoever you marry will have a lot to live up to." In her own marriage, she had not been spoiled. Now she relished going where she pleased, creating a life my father never would have fathomed.

Our first trips were group tours, but as my mother read more and saved more, we branched out on our own. We began to stay in places for those in the know—the *cognoscenti*, a word she whispered with pride. When we arrived in Venice this time, we stayed at the Flora off the Piazza San Marco. Deluxe and intimate.

The first night of our stay, the hotel made a mistake and gave us two single rooms rather than a double. The bellman unlocked doors kitty-corner from one another. Each held a narrow bed. When the dark green shutters were pushed open, one of the rooms revealed a balcony overlooking a courtyard abundant with geraniums and quiet places to sit. The other room held an ornately carved armoire, the door to which—the bellman smiled and shrugged—had to be closed if one wished to enter the bathroom.

After my mother gave the man a discreetly folded wad of lire for carrying our bags and we heard his steps echoing down the hall, we peeked into the bathroom and were surprised to see that it was huge with all new fixtures. "It's bigger than the bedrooms put together," my mother said, and we broke out laughing.

Over dinner we continued to joke about the room mix-up, but at bedtime we found ourselves unwilling to separate.

"We're being silly," she said.

"What does it matter if we're across the hall from each other?" I agreed. "We're just going to be asleep."

My mother nodded and I went to the room with the big

bathroom, giving her the one with the balcony. But a moment later I was in her room, clutching my pillow and climbing into her bed. Our shoulders knocked against each other as we lay side by side.

"Do you have enough room?" she asked.

"Yes," I lied. "Do you?"

"No," she said, and we laughed again, knowing that this would be one of the stories we'd tell when we got home. Our faces close on the smooth, white pillows, we each felt that this was what made us special, better than other mothers and daughters. We didn't want to be apart.

As we continued to wait for the train to move on from the Florence station, I surveyed the scene beyond our compartment window. My mother read her book. Danieli had his newspaper. I watched the arriving and departing passengers on the platform, picking out the Italians from the tourists. I envied the local girls with their bare, slim legs. In coy, flirty voices, dark-haired boys called to them over the heads of the milling crowd. A man with a silver cart rolled up the platform toward our end of the train. "*Dolci! Coca!*" he hawked.

"Get something if you want," my mother said from behind her green guide. Rather than her face, I saw the white letters spelling ROME across the book's cover. Even without looking at me, she knew what I was thinking.

"Are you hungry?" I asked, hoping.

"I can wait," she said. A cruel response. I wanted to be

like her—someone who needed only the passing countryside and a book to feel full. I'd already eaten the rolls that came on the hotel's room service tray that morning. She'd eaten nothing, yet I was the hungry one.

While I did not get my mother's fine nose and coloring, by the time I was twelve I had her hourglass figure. I resented having the shapeliness coveted in her era rather than the stick-figure chic of mine. Boys my age didn't know what to do with my curves, but men gave me looks that said they knew just what they wanted to do. Looks that made my mother pull me to her. I was determined to starve myself into a more controllable package—to be rail thin like the girls in the magazines I read. My determination only made me hungrier.

"I'm going to get something," I said as I quickly dug into my straw bag for my wallet.

As I rose to leave the compartment, I hesitated. Catching Danieli's eye, I wondered if he spoke English. Did he have a daughter of his own? Did he recognize these mother-daughter interactions? I stepped around his fine leather shoes and made my way down the corridor. A few moments later, I was off the train.

The platform was loud with talk and hurrying passengers as I counted out my lire for a box of cookies. Still, I recognized the first chug of our train. A tingling swarmed my legs as I looked up and saw it nudge forward. My feet would not move.

Later my mother told me that even though Danieli did not, in fact, speak English, he knew immediately what was happening. The two of them stood together to look out the window. My mother lowered the glass. She leaned out as far as she could. She saw my pink dress farther down the platform than she expected. With no time to get off the train herself, she stood there willing me to run, to jump, to leap aboard at the last minute.

~

One of the rules my mother had instilled in me on our very first trip was that if we were ever separated while traveling on a train or subway, the one left behind was to go to the next stop, where the other would be waiting. My sandals slapped the concrete as I ran toward the terminal to find another train. The schedule was on a circular stand that spun around, displaying times, track numbers, and destinations. I twirled it until I found our train. Eyes stinging with tears, I told myself I could not cry. Not until I saw my mother again. Finally, I found *ROMA* in red letters listed next to our train. That's where I would find her. Immediately below the listing, I saw another red *ROMA*.

Again, I ran. All around me, people moved like extras on a movie set, their spontaneous gestures automatic after long rehearsals: waving, kissing cheeks, buying cigarettes and magazines, bringing little cups of espresso to their lips. I followed a woman wearing a fitted suit and trailing a little boy behind her. His feet tumbled in tiny steps. A group of porters in baggy pants and gray aprons leaned on their dollies, speaking to one another, nodding, flicking cigarettes. An old one with a bear-like face said something, and two of them turned their eyes and mouths toward me. I looked away quickly and they laughed. Hugging the cookies to my chest, I wished I'd taken my passport, my bag, and my sweater from the train.

At last, breathing hard, I found the track I wanted. The conductor, a young man in a dark blue uniform dulled from too much wear, stood in the doorway.

"*Scusi, scusi,*" I said.

He lowered his clipboard and squinted at me as I tried to explain my situation. I felt tears again when I realized that he did not understand a word I was saying. I switched to my high school French. Maybe seeing my distress made him try harder, because at last we broke through to some understanding.

"*No, è pieno,*" he said.

I recognized the words. My mother and I had repeated them to each other earlier that morning, trying to imitate the finality of the Venetian ticket seller's tone when he'd told us the express train was full. It dawned on me that this train was the one we had wanted to take in the first place. This was *our* train. Our lumbering local had left much earlier, stopping several times along the way. The later departing express had arrived in Florence at the same time. I felt as if I'd bumped into someone I knew. But it was still *pieno*—full. And even if it hadn't been, all I had was a handful of purple and orange lire amounting to about nine dollars. Not enough for a ticket.

In my halting French, I tried to explain that I'd been left behind. That I had to get to *Roma*. The conductor pushed his hat higher on his forehead, listening. I can't imagine that my cobbled-together French mixed with some

English was comprehensible, but finally he shrugged. "*Avanti*," he said, stepping aside and motioning me aboard.

We passed through the first-class corridor—each compartment a blur of tortoiseshell sunglasses perched in elegant coifs, designer handbags shutting with hushed snaps. A regally bronzed woman smoothed her skirt as her husband tucked into the seat beside her, his hair a crown of silver waves. In another compartment, three well-dressed youths—high school or college age—reminded me of the flirty teens I'd seen earlier. One leaned out the window and called to someone on the platform. I noted the tilt of his hips and his broad shoulders before I caught his friend's brown eyes following me as I passed.

The conductor took me to the only empty seats on the train—in the restaurant car. Depositing me there, he said something to the waiters who were polishing glasses. Puzzling for clues to my disaster, they looked me up and down. They went back to their work as the train began to move. Relieved for the moment, I sat down at one of the tables. I watched the *Firenze* sign pass by the window. I had done it. I'd found a train. I'd followed our plan. In three hours when I reached Rome, we would be reunited. As the train barreled along, I was convinced my mother would be proud of how deftly I'd handled the situation.

But as I sped to Rome, my mother was standing on a platform in the town of Arezzo, Danieli by her side. They would wait for four trains before finally deciding that I was not coming to Arezzo, the true "next stop." Danieli did not abandon my mother. On the contrary, the old man secured passage for the two of them back to Florence on a full train with no money exchanged, and from what my mother could gather, no questions asked. They rode without speaking, sitting on jump seats attached to the wall in the engineer's car. Their luggage—*our* luggage, because my mother had mine as well—lay in a heap on the grimy floor of the big open car where men operated the train. My mother studied Danieli, trying to understand who he was and why the conductor, the train personnel, and the station policemen were all notably deferential. Was he a government official? An affluent businessman? She didn't know and never would.

As the Tuscan countryside passed me by, I couldn't help thinking that if I had kept my mouth shut the night before, none of this would have happened. It should have been the perfect evening to end our Venice stay.

To make up for the room mix-up on the first night, the hotel had given us a gorgeous suite. Mornings, we'd breakfasted in the little garden we'd seen the first day. We'd been to St. Mark's Basilica, Doge's Palace, and the opera at *Teatro La Fenice*. For our final dinner, my mother chose one of the best restaurants in the city— La Caravella.

A man in a beautiful suit had been seated at the table next to ours. Sitting on the banquette beside my mother, dining alone, he soon struck up a conversation with us. The divide between our tables seemed to disappear a little more with each course until it was as if the three of us were enjoying the meal together. Between the veal *carpaccio* and risotto with fennel, he leaned nearer to her. By the oven-roasted turbot, he'd touched her elbow twice. His hair was thin, but he had nice teeth. As the dark chocolate mousse arrived, he began telling a charming story that was supposedly meant for me while his eyes addressed her.

After we left the restaurant, I started the argument, keeping it in until we were walking down the hall back to our room. "Why do you talk to them?" I demanded even as I tried to keep my voice low so other guests behind their closed doors wouldn't hear.

"I was just being polite," my mother said, sliding the heavy key into the hotel room door.

"It's like you don't even know what they want." I spat the words at her. I'm not sure what made me angrier. That she seemed to glide around, oblivious to her charms, responding to these men as if she had no clue about the effect she was having on them. Or that she never used these charms to close the deal, marry again, and be like everyone else's mother.

"I believe I know a thing or two," she said, stepping out of her *peau de soie* heels and sinking to the floor in stocking feet.

"Not lately," I said. We both knew what I meant. When was the last time she'd been on a date? She'd had one relationship when I was in elementary school and that was it. If she knew so much about being with men, I certainly hadn't seen any evidence of it.

"And why do you suppose that is?" She stared at me.

Was she saying that if I hadn't been there she would have

pursued the flirtations of the man in the restaurant? In that moment I saw his hand at the small of her back, guiding her as they strolled to one of the little cafés on the square. Or perhaps on their way to a Campari and soda in the bar of his hotel. From there, who knew?

Not once had I ever heard her openly rue our situation. Never had I heard her say she wished to be free of me even for an evening. Was she finally saying it was my fault that she was still alone? Didn't she know that's what I worried about most: that I'd kept her from a happy life? Afraid of what she might say next, I went into the bathroom to brush my teeth.

When I came out, I saw she had gone out to the balcony. Still in her dinner dress, she stood looking at the building tops and dark sky. I watched her for a moment. I knew if I gave her the chance she'd take back what she'd said. She'd say I was the best thing that had ever happened to her, like she always did. But sometimes that made it worse, because her life never looked like enough to me. I knew that as her constant companion, I must hold her back. I wanted more for her and for me.

I climbed into bed, turning my face to the wall. As I drifted asleep, I imagined not for the first time, what it would have been like for her if she'd never had me. Would she have gone back to college after divorcing my father? Would she have become the photojournalist she'd longed to be as a girl? Would she have found a traveling companion truly worthy of her? For years, before that night and after, I daydreamed an alternate life for my mother, pictured her living abroad, walking down cobblestone streets arm in arm with a man who treasured her. How often I worried that, in the end, I would be the love of her life.

We woke the next morning to a knock on the door and the morning's breakfast tray. Realizing we'd overslept, we rushed to the station only to find the train we'd hoped to take was full—the train I was now riding to Rome.

⁓

At one o'clock, the dining car began filling with the first-class passengers I'd seen earlier. The bronze woman and the silver-haired man sat at a table nearby. My appetite had left with my mother's train, but now as I smelled sauces finessed with wine and saw baskets of bread being served, knowing that I seemed to have righted my situation, I felt free to be hungry again. Yet surely the conductor had not meant for me to eat. Waiting for someone to tell me to leave, I looked out the window at the yellow fields and distant hills rolling by.

I heard the plate being placed on the table before I saw it. "*Antipasto*," the waiter said, smiling. "*Scampi*." Three large shrimp stared at me; their orange bodies, with fountain-like feelers and black eyes, were arranged prettily on the plate. He nodded for me to try them. "Zrimps. Very good." He moved on to the next table.

As I cut into the sweet, chewy shrimp, the three young men I'd seen earlier entered the dining car. They scanned the car, and somehow I knew they'd come looking for me. I sat up straighter, pretending not to notice at first. They were not the shy boys I was used to from home. After they spotted me, they gathered around like birds hopping closer to a park bench. Their leader, who introduced himself as Claudio, pointed to the chairs at my table. All it took was a dip of my head, the slightest signal of yes, and they were seated beside me. I saw the elegantly tanned older woman frown at the scene. Claudio was lanky with dark curls, brows, and lashes. His prominent Adam's apple showed above his collared shirt tucked into slim jeans. His friends had the names of other Shakespearean characters—Mercutio and Antonio.

"American?" he asked. I'd barely said a word. What was it about me that conveyed this? I'd always had the feeling that Europeans regarded Americans as children playing at being grown-ups.

"Californian," I said. "From where they make the movies." My mother often said this when we were making chitchat with strangers we met on our trips. It sounded dumb coming from me, but Claudio didn't seem to think so. "Ah, Hollywood," he said, as if I'd already confided something special to him.

When the waiter brought their appetizers, they ordered wine, which startled me. I'd only had champagne on New Year's Eve and at weddings. After the wine arrived, Claudio poured some into my glass. I lifted it to my lips and he watched me drink.

He knew only a little English. His friends knew even less. But together we made our way through two more courses—veal battered and fried to golden with flecks of black pepper, lemon wedges fanned in a pinwheel beside it, followed by a dessert of berries and *zabaglione*. Through the meal, I gleaned from Claudio that he had two sisters. That he lived in Florence. That he was in his first year at university.

I was exotic to them. That was clear as I tucked my hair behind my ear, aware of the way they took in my moves with appreciation. Under their gaze, I felt a swirl of pride rather than embarrassment at the display of my breasts beneath my summery pink dress.

After the plates were cleared, Claudio leaned across the table, hunkering down for more conversation. It seemed impossibly intimate to be near enough to see where he had shaved away his dark beard. I pictured him standing in front of a mirror, shirtless. I heard the scrape of the razor against his handsome jaw. When he asked me how old I was, I didn't know numbers in Italian but I lied with my hands, counting out seventeen instead of fifteen.

Claudio had somehow made it clear to his friends that I was his. Either through one of their lilting Italian exchanges or simply because he was in charge, they seemed to have agreed that after the meal the others would go back to their compartment while he stayed.

I was glad when they left. I tried not to look at Claudio too often, but each time I did I found him watching me, too. Perhaps it was the power I felt when I lifted my glass and let the wine with its buttery softness slide over my tongue and down my throat. Perhaps it was the fact that even though I'd been separated from my mother I was okay. Whatever it was, as the train moved forward, I felt like the figurehead on a ship pushing into my future.

Claudio lit a cigarette. One brown eye squinted as he blew the smoke upward. I reached for the little box of matches he'd laid on the table. We listened to the matchsticks rattle in the box as I turned it end over end. I imagined telling my mother about him. Already I'd envisioned him picking me up for a date at our hotel in Rome. We would sit beside each other in a taxi, or even better, one of those carriages you could hire. We'd sit beside each other the way my mother and I had in the gondola. As he brought his cigarette to his lips, I realized I was afraid to kiss someone who smoked. But I told myself that I would. Maybe I would even smoke, myself.

Then Claudio said, "*Napoli*? You go to *Napoli*?"

"Naples?" I didn't understand.

"*Si, si.* Tonight holiday." He pronounced it like *holy-day*. "Big party. *Bell'assai.* Lights. Singing." How could we not have covered this ground earlier? Until that moment, it had never occurred to me that he might be going anywhere but Rome.

He leaned toward me again. "You will come?" He asked this almost in a whisper. He *does* like me, I thought. He does.

Then I thought, *Just one more stop.* All I had to do was stay on the train. I pushed the idea of my frantic mother out of my head. *Just one more stop.* I could go to *Napoli* with Claudio and come back that night. I could tell my mother that I had made a mistake; the train didn't stop in Rome. I had to go all the way to Naples and come back. The train people were nice. They'd helped me even though I had no money. I was almost sixteen. Not that much younger than she'd been when she married my father. I wasn't going to make a mistake like that. No, I only wanted Claudio to kiss me. I only wanted to feel his boy-man arms hold me.

"But I have to come back tonight," I said, the thrill of "yes" on my lips.

"Tonight. Yes. Tonight, *Ahn-dre-ah*," he said, letting each vowel in my name linger in his mouth.

⌒

As we neared Rome, the fields and hills gave way to factories and suburbs. Claudio had returned to his compartment to tell his friends I would be going with them. Would they clap him on the back, exchange a knowing smile? Would they envy him? I didn't want to think too carefully about what I was doing.

"*Roma. Fra poco.*"

I turned from the window to see the young conductor who had let me on the train. He gestured outside. "*Roma,*" he said again.

"*Si,*" I nodded. "*Si.*" I knew he was telling me to get ready—that Rome was the next stop. I thanked him and watched him move down the aisle. As soon as he'd gone, I headed in the opposite direction. I found the restroom and shut myself inside.

Flushed from the wine, I leaned close to the spotty little mirror above the sink. I ran a brown paper towel across it, hoping to get a better look. I wanted, as always, to understand how people saw me. My father's almond, deep-set eyes. My mother's cheekbones and her strong jaw, always a little defiant. My nose too broad to make me beautiful.

I bit my lips and watched them redden. Raising an eyebrow at my image, I saw that my looks were not equal to my mother's. Her desirability did not have to be guessed at. But remembering how Claudio had said my name, I relished having an appeal all my own.

The train was slowing now, arriving in Rome. I went back to the restaurant car, hoping Claudio would be there, but the car was empty. Even the waiters were gone. I passed by our table and noticed my box of cookies still on a chair. Tucking the box under my arm, I made my way to the open train door and stepped down the high metal steps. In the moments I'd studied myself in the mirror, I'd admitted the truth to myself. Naples wasn't what I wanted. I wasn't ready for that. Instead, it was enough to know that Claudio wanted me to go with him. It was enough to know that if I wanted to I could.

My mother couldn't possibly be in Rome yet, but I scanned the crowd on the platform anyway. As I headed toward the station, I heard the express train, now bound for Naples, start to lumber forward. Then I heard my name: "*Ahn-dre-ah.*" Turning, I saw Claudio leaning out his window. "*Ahn-dre-ah,*" he said again with a question on his face. I smiled and waved at him. "*Ahn-dre-ah,* marry me, *Ahn-dre-ah,*" he called as he sailed by.

❧

My mother and Danieli had searched the Florence station for me. They'd talked to the police there. They'd gone back to Arezzo. Finally, Danieli suggested they go on to Rome. It was nearly midnight when they arrived. My mother and I had been separated for ten hours.

It was Danieli who saw me first. I was sitting on a circular bench in the center of the station, hunched forward, elbows on knees. He dropped his brown satchel and reached for my mother's elbow. He tipped his head in my direction. He and my mother had been managing in this silent way all day. His fingers slipped from her arm as she moved in long strides toward me.

"Where was *I*? Where were *you*?" she said, finally releasing me. She pretended her tone was playful, but she seemed grateful when the old man wagged his head, scolding me over the grief I'd caused her: "Andrea, Andrea, Andrea." Neither of them could know that I liked hearing my name with the *ahs* that Claudio had used.

"I went to the next stop," I said. "Rome." I waved my hand at the station around us. Did my mother notice the color in my cheeks? As I tried to defend myself, did she catch a glimmer of guilt over what I'd been tempted to do with Claudio?

"Arezzo was the next stop," she said evenly, but her breath was high and tight at the back of her throat. "We waited and waited." I could see her panic returning.

"The train schedule said Rome." I looked from my mother to Danieli. I knew I wouldn't convince them that I'd done the right thing.

"It doesn't matter," she said, quickly tamping down her fear again. Later, when we finally made it to our hotel in Rome, she would drink both the bottle and the split of champagne in the room's minibar.

I didn't remind them that I had been waiting, too. First for our original slow train to arrive, expecting my mother to emerge from it. Then when she hadn't, I'd posted myself on a central bench, believing that she would find me eventually. Hours later, she had.

The three of us stood in a little circle until I reached for my straw bag, which my mother had been carrying.

"Shall we?" she said at last.

Danieli adjusted his leather case over his shoulder. "*Andiamo*," he said.

We walked to the station's ornate open entryway. Taxis lined the curb. Usually the drivers made me nervous with their hovering, their urgent vying to be chosen. That night we were not pestered. The old man steered us to the first cab in line and said something to the driver.

Danieli, whose real name we never learned, held the taxi door open for us. Once we were inside, he gently closed it, remaining protectively by the window. Then he bowed the way he had when he first entered our train compartment. I waved at him. My mother's face was turned to the window, so I could not see her expression. But I hoped she was rewarding him with another of her beautiful smiles. As the cab pulled away, we leaned back against the seat, reunited, our shoulders not quite touching.

The
Wolf
and
the
Lamb

A FEW BLOCKS FROM SUNSET BOULEVARD IN HIS WHITE
stucco house perched on a hill, my father looks into the mirror above his bathroom sink. I imagine him taking in the
shape of his head, his jaw, and the worth of each profile. He
does this in one sweeping, practiced glance. He's learned not
to lean in close, not to bring into focus the scribble of red
lines that began forming across the top of each chiseled
cheekbone after he hit forty.

He empties six ice trays into the sink's basin and takes a
deep breath before plunging his face into the cold. Paul
Newman taught him the ice trick a dozen years before, when
they met on a movie set. Back when Nick's future was
stretching out before him and the preservation of his looks
was a serious matter.

He pulls his face from the ice and pats it dry. Tossing the
towel around his neck, he goes into his bedroom and stares
into the closet, surveying the contents. He selects his navy
Dunhill blazer, a pair of tan slacks, and a pale blue shirt. He

reaches in for one of three pairs of Gucci loafers, the pair that has held up the best. He never wears the others, but he keeps them because he likes the look of more.

It makes a certain kind of sense that he became an actor. His father owned the Pontiac dealership in their midsize Texas town. His granddaddy was a wildcatter in the oil fields. Each profession required its own brand of optimism and charm.

But Nick's optimism has started to flag. His recent television pilot didn't sell, and lately callbacks are few and far between. His second wife left him around the time his agent stopped calling.

While my father has been up and down on his luck several times since my mother left him, this time—broke and single again—he finally decides to track us down.

∞

It had been sixteen years and my mother had hidden us well. We'd moved far from where my parents first met. She'd distanced us further with a new last name. So when Nick came looking for us again, he had to do some detective work.

He started with the California Department of Motor Vehicles. He told the clerk he was my grandfather. He said he couldn't read the expiration date on his license. This was the late 1970s, before identity protection was a priority. The clerk happily looked up my grandfather's license. No doubt my father said: "Now, darlin',"—or "pal," depending on the clerk's gender—"what address do you have down there in your files?

Let's make sure you've got the right one." And just like that, he had my grandfather's latest address.

Address in hand, he called information and got my grandfather's phone number. From there, my mother and I were just a step away.

I'm not sure what lie my father would have told if my grandfather, who despised him, had answered the phone. But when he called, my grandfather's second wife was the only one home.

I bet it surprised Nick when a woman other than my grandmother answered. My grandparents were the type who seemed like they would stay together forever. But when I was still in elementary school, my grandmother had shown up at our door one evening. She'd made the three-hour drive from Fresno to Los Angeles. After thirty-one years of marriage, she'd left my grandfather.

She slept on our couch, slowly revealing the truth to my mother. My grandmother might not have wanted to see the world like her daughter, but she didn't want to settle for a constrained life either. She'd been having an affair with my grandfather's best friend, who was younger than my grandfather, had more money, and laughed more.

Ultimately, after staying with us for a few months and then getting an apartment of her own until the divorce went through a year later, she married him. She wore a powder blue suit, matching pillbox hat with a little veil, and an orchid wrist corsage. My mother made the three-tiered wedding cake.

My grandfather married again too. His second wife wasn't as smart as my grandmother, and she had no reason to be wary of smooth-talking men who said they were old friends of the family. When Nick told her he'd gone to high school with my mother and wanted to catch up, she helpfully gave him my mother's office number.

It was the summer between my junior and senior years of high school. I still spent my vacation working at my mother's law firm. I'd graduated from stamping legal pads to reconciling bank accounts and messengering documents to the courthouse. When the phone rang that day, my mother and I had just finished lunch. We were sitting in her big office with a view of the Hollywood Sign in the distance. From across the desk, I saw her close her eyes as she took in Nick's hello. Later, I would wonder how a person could so easily recognize a voice not heard in over a decade.

She stood up from her desk, pushing her chair back so it rolled across the plastic mat beneath it. "We don't need anything from you," she said. She was proud. Proud of all she'd accomplished. Proud of who we were.

Perhaps she'd always known this call would come and was relieved to finally get it over with. Perhaps she was grateful that he'd left us alone long enough for me to be almost grown. I think we'd both been waiting all those years for him to find us. All I can say for sure is that, as I watched my mother speak to my father, I wanted to know what he was offering. I wanted to know in the same way one is tempted by street peddlers whose coat linings gleam with deals too good to be true. As my mother stared out the window, she already knew how much I wanted to see him.

Cautiously, a few negotiating calls later, she set a time

and place for my father and me to meet. It was her idea to be there, too, hidden from view. She would not come between us, but she would be there to protect me if things got out of hand.

"What do you think might happen?" I asked. Was it just that he could say something mean or upsetting? Or did she fear for my physical safety—imagine him clapping one hand over my mouth and dragging me away?

"I just need to be there," she said.

Although I'd seen him on television, my father was not someone I would have recognized if I'd passed him on the street. Even on TV, I'd confused him with the young Nick Nolte in the miniseries *Rich Man, Poor Man*. I'd wondered if he was the handsome major on the old *Lost in Space* show. But on the terrace of the restaurant where we met, I instantly knew him. And he knew me.

As soon as I came into the sunlight, he stood up. Was it his mother's red hair he recognized or his own dark, squinting eyes? Maybe he glimpsed my mother in me—a resemblance that was becoming more pronounced the older I got. Did he see a quick mirage of her face in mine? He fingered the single button on his sport coat as he watched me walk toward him.

The time it took me to reach the table was excruciating, too long for him to be studying me. In his navy blazer and tan slacks, he was thinner than the beefy youth I'd seen posing in a championship baseball uniform. My mother kept a box of old photos on the living room shelf that had always put me in a black mood whenever I shuffled through them— her smiling homecoming princess face heading to her doom, his posturing bravado. Moving around the table now, his wiry frame made him seem slight even at the six feet I knew him to be.

"Hello, darlin'." He laid his hand on my arm as if I'd always been his. When he bent to kiss my cheek, there was something silvery in his scent—metallic yet honeyed, like sweet bells. I wondered if this was the cologne my mother had always spoken of. Despite the Gucci loafers and gold signet ring, his East Texas twang remained.

When he pulled my chair out, I remembered to half-sit until the seat was fully under me. My insides fidgeted while he stood behind me. What imperfections might he see back there? In the ladies' room a few minutes before, I'd only thought to check my front.

Across the table, he chewed on the corner of his mouth, pursing his lips and smiling at the same time. Then he smiled wider. Under his gaze and the perfect white of his teeth, I sat straighter, the thin straps of my sundress going taut against my collarbones each time I took a breath.

As he watched me, the tip of his tongue darted to the inside of his cheek, poking it, making me think he was on the edge of speaking.

Unable to stand it any longer, I burst out, "What?"

"Well, all I can say is it's a good thing I didn't run into you in a bar. I might've hit on you."

My mother would not have liked him saying that. Not at

all. But I smiled. I'd always been a bit player in their story, but in that moment I stepped on stage. He seemed to be telling me that I not only measured up to her—someone he had also wanted—but I was worthy of being the product of the two of them, my larger-than-life parents. With that wrong thing, my father had said just the right thing.

As I sat eating my chicken Caesar salad and he his turkey club, he smirked between bites, taking me in. We talked about movies. He was delighted that I'd seen the classic Gregory Peck western *Yellow Sky*. "Everyone has seen *Giant* and *Treasure of the Sierra Madre*. But *Yellow Sky*—now that's an all-time great."

He told me how, when he was in his twenties, *On the Road* had inspired him to hitchhike down to Mexico and out to New York City, where he'd crashed on Sammy Davis Jr.'s couch. "Betcha didn't know that about your old man, did you?" Neither of us said the obvious—I didn't know much about my old man, period.

He'd met the Beatles while shooting a movie in Copenhagen. Like Hemingway, he'd been to Spain for the running of the bulls. I didn't know how much to believe, but I wanted to believe, and clearly he wanted to impress.

Then he leaned in conspiratorially. "Now, tell me, are you a good girl?"

"I get good grades, if that's what you mean."

"Oh, that's right, you'll be going to a fancy college pretty soon." Wanting to impress him, too, I'd told him about my plans for after high school.

"And you do what your mother tells you, I suppose?"

"It's not like that." I took a sip of my iced tea. "She trusts me. She doesn't need to tell me what to do."

He nodded as if he understood, but I didn't see how he could. What did he know about having a daughter?

"She was like that," he said. "Did what her parents wanted. Until she met me, of course." He said this proudly, laughing, as if I was supposed to find my mother's downfall and his role in it endearing. "Not me, though. My folks had to get after me. Sent me to military school twice."

"Somehow I knew that."

He smiled, biting his cheek again. "But you know . . ." His gaze flicked toward me. "Those good girls."

"What?"

"Those good girls—they're the ones who really want it. They're the horny ones."

"Gross." I felt my face go hot. I was giving him the reaction he wanted, and he was enjoying it.

"It's true." He laughed. "Ask her."

It was the "ask her" that got to me as I watched my father gobble up another bite of sandwich. In all my mother's stories, I'd always seen her as the lamb headed to slaughter. But behind my blush, I knew he was right. We good girls did want it—I knew that from afternoons I'd spent in my room with my boyfriend before my mother came home from work. It was he who'd had to stop us from going all the way, he who hadn't been ready for the force of my good girl's desire.

I imagined the secrets my mother must have kept from her parents. The way these secrets made her feel reckless but powerful too. And then I could see it, my mother as the young beauty in all her photos, my father's breath on her ear, stirring her desire. The story of the lamb taken in by the wolf began to shift in my mind. The two of them, how amazed they were that his arm could circle all the way around her waist. How sometimes, in the middle of her undoing, he would draw back, awed just to look at her. The lamb's teeth sharpened as she moved in to kiss him, his wolf's fur soft and plush to the touch.

I saw my mother then, the sixteen-year-old good girl greeting her parents, swinging schoolbooks onto one hip, her fine legs carrying her smoothly on her way. Secret pride in his desire for her making her smile. Surely, this was love.

It was only later, after they married and she was far from her parents' house, that the arms that encircled her waist would sometimes refuse to let go, squeezing tighter until the lamb was wild with the need to breathe. He'd snap her head back, gripping her skull in one large hand. *Who did she think she was,* he accused through gritted teeth. All because she'd said hello to a valet who'd opened her car door or because she'd been late home from work. "But I love you," she'd need to say again and again, the words like a lion tamer's chair holding back the beast. "I love you," she'd say again. Only then would his grip loosen.

When lunch was over, I waited in the ladies' room until Nick left the restaurant. My mother, who'd been watching us from across the patio through the potted palms, green eyes narrowed, came to collect me.

On the way home in the car, after a long silence, I finally said, "He was nice."

"Oh, I didn't think he'd be anything but captivating."

"You didn't?"

She looked at me. "It's his way." Turning back to the road, she seemed to see all the miles behind us and all the miles ahead. "He takes you in with casual charm and easy persuasion." She seemed surprised that I hadn't understood this.

I didn't mention the way he sat across from me with his knowing pursed-lip smile. The one that made me look away and laugh. I didn't tell her what he'd said about hitting on me. But as we drove on, I played the scene in my mind. I pictured myself mingling in the kind of upscale bars my father no doubt frequented. Despite my pale skin and baby-fat features, in my imagination I was smooth and comfortable. From among the tanned California girls with their bare midriffs and slim white pants, he chose me.

⌒

I took up with my father hungrily, in the way of new romance. Even my appetite evaporated like that of someone in love. I grew very thin in a matter of days. My mother gave me time off from my summer job to be with him. While she worked, Nick took me to ball games at Dodger Stadium, where we sat in box seats. We went to The Daisy on Rodeo Drive, The Ivy on Robertson, Dan Tana's on Santa Monica Boulevard, and the Polo Lounge at the Beverly Hills Hotel. He knew everyone everywhere. We never sat down to eat. He was always just "stopping by to see a buddy." He'd keep his gold-rimmed Porsche aviators on and order a beer. He'd introduce me

proudly, saying, "Isn't she pretty?" Sometimes, he'd buy me a
Coke and say, "Get something if you want," but I wasn't hungry.
I was sated in a way I had never been. He was my Rosetta
Stone, the clue I'd been missing all my life. Here was the
source of my athleticism, quick temper, and big feet. Here
were my brown eyes with flecks of green staring back at me.
As close as I'd always been to my mother, I never felt we were
cut from the same cloth. My grandparents had often compared us: As a child, my mother had been a delicate, quiet
reader lost in books for hours, but my childhood nickname
had been "Motor Mouth." "We always knew exactly where
you were," my grandfather would say.

While my mother's early teenage years looked like an
episode of *Happy Days*, mine seemed more like an *ABC After-
school Special*. She had been valedictorian and homecoming
queen. Her portrait hung in two photography store-
fronts—the beauty in the window that the most popular boys
in school rushed to ask out.

I struggled through anything that wasn't a humanities
class, and I'd had one boyfriend. He was the only guy who
paid real attention to me in a high school where cool girls
were blond and bronzed. Bespectacled and with the begin-
nings of a dark, downy mustache, he sat in the back of our
honors classes making sex jokes with his friends. The other
girls called him a "perv." I kept my make-out sessions with
him secret not only from my mother but also from my friends
before finally dropping him, ashamed of what I wanted to do
with him.

If he had been more acceptable in the eyes of my peers,

would I have been as embarrassed by what I wanted? Was it my worry over being "loose?" Or was it that I didn't have a more appealing partner in crime the way my mother had? I've often thought if I had known we were so alike—good girls who could be overcome by their desires—I would have felt more comfortable in my own skin long ago.

I had figured that the reason my mother didn't keep me from seeing the man we'd been hiding from for so long was simply that she'd gotten tired of being on guard. That she thought he could no longer hurt us. But that wasn't it. That wasn't it at all.

It took about a month before they could stand it no longer. A month before I understood that the days I'd spent with my father had been an odd kind of foreplay to the time when my mother would lie beside him again.

It started with a dinner to which I was not invited. I'd learn later that he'd been asking her out almost since that first call. She'd held him off but eventually agreed. "We just need to talk," she told me. "Clear the air."

I didn't hear them come in after dinner. But the next morning, I just knew what I'd find. I crept out to our living room and there they were—entwined on our couch. She would tell me later that the couch—rather than her bed—was her concession to me. But I also saw it as a last-ditch attempt to deny what she'd been wanting all along.

Seeing them together, what *I* wanted was to hurt her. I

slipped out the front door and ran. I wanted her to wake up, find me gone, and worry. I hoped she'd be sick about it.

When she finally found me a few hours later, I was sitting on a park bench. I hoped she'd searched all over, racked her brain to figure out where I'd gone, called all my friends looking for me.

She approached carefully, the way you might close in on an unbridled horse.

"You said you hated him." I spoke without looking at her.

"I know," she said. She moved closer.

"You said he was violent and vicious."

"I know," she said. She continued to creep forward until she sat beside me.

On their date, Nick had taken her to an Italian place popular with celebrities. He'd taken me there as well. When she scooted closer to me on the bench, she put her arms around me, sideways, her face very close to mine. As she tried to draw me in tighter, I smelled her breath reeking of garlic.

"Your breath. It's horrible," was all I would say. Quickly, she pulled back.

"I'm sorry," she said, her hand to her mouth. "I'm sorry," she said again, both of us knowing her breath was the least of it.

❧

I'd so rarely seen my mother with a man. I'd known her to have only one other real romance, back when I was in elementary school. He was a married lawyer who came to our apartment after I was supposed to be in bed for the night. Before he arrived, she would change from her secretary dresses and pantyhose into what she called a hostess gown or lounging pajamas—elegant clothes my Uncle Don, who managed a department store, got her at a discount. I remember in particular a pair of beautiful raspberry-colored pants and a matching blouse with rhinestone buttons.

Even at eight or nine years old, I understood that she and this man must be having a physical relationship, but I never saw them touch each other. No kissing, hugging, snuggling, lap sitting, even when I caught them off guard as I tiptoed into the living room, curious about their brandy snifters and the meals she made for him with names like *coq au vin*.

Their affair went on for three years. I knew that my mother and I—each in her own way—dreamed that one day he would leave his wife and children. Finally, he did separate from his family, moving into an apartment in Marina del Rey, where all divorced fathers seemed to live. From his deck, you could see white sailboats moored in a row of slips.

One school night we went to his place. While I did my homework, my mother made dinner in his efficiency kitchen. The two of them talked as he sat on a barstool across the counter from her, drinking scotch, still in his charcoal-gray suit pants, monogrammed shirt, and silk tie.

After dinner I watched television in his bedroom while they stayed in the living room sipping amber liquid. At some point I must have fallen asleep. I woke to the man sitting at the edge of the bed, telling me that everything was okay but my mother wasn't feeling well. That we'd be staying the night.

Behind him I could see her standing in the hallway, her naked body so white it almost glowed. She weaved slightly. He called to her a soothing, "It's okay. She's okay." I'd never seen my mother drunk. I'd never seen her out of control like that. But even in her condition she was compelled to check on me. He tried to block my view of her, wanting to protect us both.

I was never sure why she and the lawyer broke up, but I didn't see her undone like that again until my father came back into our lives. I think now that's why she kept men at bay during most of my childhood. It wasn't that she didn't want them, didn't yearn to have them love her as much as I wanted such love. It was that the men she loved couldn't be trusted. They said they loved you, but even after they left their wives they didn't marry you. They said they loved you, but then they turned dangerous and possessive.

My mother was sheepish about taking up with my father again. Other than that first morning when I'd seen them on the couch, they kept their physical affections mostly hidden from me. But one night that same summer, when just the two of us were heading home from work and we stood waiting for the elevator, a bright drop of blood splattered to the marble floor between her feet.

"Oh my god," she said. She dug in her purse for a tissue and wiped it away. "I'll be back," she said, heading for the ladies' room. When she returned, she pushed the elevator button again. "I'm sorry," she said. "That was so embarrassing." She watched the light above the elevator door making its way to our floor. When at last it dinged and the doors slid open, we stepped inside. As the doors closed, she said to me, "It must be the IUD."

She was only thirty-six at the time. It stunned me to think they could actually have another child if they wanted to. They could actually get married and do it all again.

Reading
the
Signs

IN THE BEGINNING, I HANDLED MY PARENTS' REUNION by turning it into a story. We all did. Nick was no longer the villain, but rather he and my mother were star-crossed lovers.

From my mother's point of view, if she ended up with my father it meant she'd never been wrong to choose him in the first place. Nick said they were like the twice-married movie stars Natalie Wood and Robert Wagner; that was before the actress drowned off Catalina Island and her husband became the chief suspect.

Knowing I would be leaving for college soon, I convinced myself that my mother might finally be taken care of— might finally have her life happily ever after so I could move on to find mine.

Like children playing house, we took on cardboard cutout roles: *You be mother. You be father. And I'll be the baby.* My mother dragged out that box of mementos that used to be on our living room shelf—the one with the pressed prom corsages and the wedding album that had always depressed me. At some point, she'd stuffed it under her bed along with a pink suitcase filled with my old *Nancy Drew*s and international doll collection.

Among the photos were a few of me as a baby when we still lived in Las Vegas. In one, all you could see were Nick's arms holding me high above his head as he lay back on their bed. My mother had once told me that later that day he'd gone to Galveston, Texas, with friends. It was "Splash Day," when the Texas beaches opened for Spring Break. He'd left my mother alone to care for me while he played beach blanket bingo with co-eds.

The three of us gazed at the photos together. Instead of hearing her stories about his jealousy and her bruises, they reminisced about the baby shower thrown for her by Nick's friends. They left out the part about his not allowing her to invite her own friends. These were the scraps from which my parents and I created a shared history.

I began calling him "Dad," even though the feel of the word in my mouth was as foreign as a new language. I'd find excuses to say it in the grocery store, at a ball game, at the dinner table. "Did you hear me?" I'd ask.

"I heard you," he snapped one day. "But if you have to say something about it every time, what's the point?"

Didn't he know the gift I was bestowing on him—the honor of holding that title, especially now that I knew his return had always been about my mother? Perhaps those harsh words of his were the first sign of things to come.

❧

The summer Nick came back into our lives, my mother had already scheduled our most ambitious trip yet—a two-week cruise around the Greek islands followed by another two weeks in Egypt. He began to sulk as our departure date approached. The night before we left, we opened the apartment door to find him standing on the welcome mat, hands tucked into the front pockets of his jeans, smirking as if we couldn't have guessed who it was.

My mother—still wearing a silk dress from work—kissed him on the cheek and turned back to pondering her open suitcase on the bed. He followed close behind. As she flitted from dresser to closet, he grabbed her around the middle before she sailed by. From my perch on the velvet settee in her bedroom, I watched as he wouldn't let go. "Will you stop," she finally laughed, meaning it but also keeping her voice light.

Banished to the opposite corner of the settee, he reached an arm my way, screwing a finger into my rib cage to tickle my side until I laugh-cried and clamped my elbow down to make it stop. He teased her about the men who'd be after her on the trip. When she rolled her eyes, he shrugged without making eye contact and said, "That's okay, I'll be here waiting." Unbeknownst to me, after I went to bed, he asked her to marry him.

As we toured the Parthenon, tried ouzo, and took each other's photo at Olympia, site of the first Olympics, she silently considered her answer. If she asked the oracle at Delphi for guidance, she didn't share it with me. Only later did she tell me she would have accepted his proposal if it hadn't been for what happened soon after our return.

Part of me wishes I could remember the exact moment Nick got comfortable enough to let down his guard. When did he decide he no longer had to sell us on the kinder, gentler him? Or maybe he just got tired of not knowing where he stood. My mother held all the cards as he waited for her to give him her answer.

School had started again, and Nick took to picking me up most afternoons. He'd take me back to his house to watch movies. The house was modest, but its location with a view of the Hollywood Hills made it special. From the driveway, you could also see Sunset Boulevard below.

Nick's décor was mostly baseball memorabilia. Friends with many of the L.A. Dodgers—Garvey, Buckner, Yeager— he had winning bats and signed balls displayed in a rack over the television. Around them hung photos chronicling his life after my mother had left him. A brief stint with the Pittsburgh Pirates farm team, headshots from his modeling days in New York City, a Pan Am ad campaign he'd done with his second wife, who was also a model.

As *Cool Hand Luke* or *The Great Escape* flickered on-screen, we sat on his big leather couch and ate from a stack of Sara Lee chocolate cream pies he kept in the freezer. He dissected Steve McQueen's acting and John Huston's directing. That's when he explained how Paul Newman submerged his face in a bowl of ice each morning to stay looking young.

As he switched from pie to beer, he took to schooling me on other kinds of facts. In his precise Kilgore, Texas, diction, he'd say: "Here's the thing, Andrea. The thing you should know. No one knows your mother better than I do. Not her parents. Not you. She has *always* loved me. Never stopped. Not since she was sixteen."

I'd nod. The next day or the day after, he'd tell me again. "I never stopped loving her and it was the same for her."

Each of these declarations was a tiny crack in the fragile story we'd all cooked up. During one of those conversations did my face give me away? Did I give him an "if-you-say-so" shrug? Longing to say, "But, but, wait, what about the fact that you were an asshole to her? What about how you bullied and threatened her?" Part of him must have known how much I wanted to say, "Nah ah, she loves *me* more." But I bit my tongue.

Maybe I finally baited him. Perhaps as he got more comfortable, coiled more deeply into the corner of the couch, and drank not one or two beers but three or four, his placid veneer crashed under the weight of all the little cracks in our story. One thing I know for sure: Since the day I'd met him, I'd been both afraid and excited to see if the vicious man my mother had described would ever show himself to me.

One day, he did.

If I'd been paying attention, I might have caught the exact moment he wasn't playing anymore. I would learn to recognize the signs soon enough. I would come to sense them the way a deer suddenly stills, looking up from the grass it's been nibbling, ears pricked, sniffing the air for fire.

That first time, it likely started with a glance in my direction, as if he couldn't quite believe the words that had just come out of my mouth. Disgusted, he would have looked away. He may have rapped his gold Tiffany signet ring against the brown glass of his beer bottle—reminding me that his gnarled hands had broken many faces. In the years to come, I would worry that those hands would pound me, too. The fear of that kept the air buzzing between us. I think he counted on it.

I would come to understand that the more he drank, the more injustices and hurts he internally catalogued: Why hadn't I taken my shoes off when entering the house as he'd told me to? How dare I resent that he'd waited so long to show an interest in me. With his dead eyes and tense jaw, finally he would decide it was his turn to get back at me for these crimes. Then he would spring, saying whatever cutting remark came to mind. The uglier the better.

That first time he began to rage at me, he might as well have had me in his jaws shaking the life out of me. Accordingly, I went limp. I don't remember everything he said. I can only offer examples from the store of barbs he hurled at me from then on:

"I bet you have those pale pink nipples. Am I right?" At seventeen, I would wonder if such nipples were bad, the least preferred.

"That shirt makes you look like a cow. Are you sure you're not pregnant? Just fat, I guess."

"You just don't get it, do you? I'm a helluva lot smarter than you are."

When he said these things, he'd stand over me—hands tucked into the pockets of his jeans, shoulders slouched and casual. Then he'd fling an arm out as if to say *the hell with you* as he delivered the final blow: "You don't fuckin' deserve to be in the same room with me." He'd point at me. "Get out of my sight. Did you hear me? Get out of my sight!"

Later, I would boil with my own rage—didn't he know he was the one who didn't deserve me?

The night of that first outburst, my mother found me whimpering in Nick's bathroom. She'd arrived and seen him passed out on the couch and me nowhere in sight. She'd finally found me sitting on the bathroom tiles, my back against the wall, still spent from sobbing and trying to make sense of the irony that I'd been out of his sight almost all my life.

After that, I understood better how my mother at sixteen had been taken in by him. I'd just as eagerly, just as willingly gone down those dark basement steps, hoping to find love at the bottom. I wanted this father of mine with my whole heart. But the Nick who at first had done everything he could to make me love him—that Nick disappeared that day. I rarely saw him ever again. Oh, the handsome charmer remained. It was just those dead eyes I had to watch out for.

⌒

Memory is a tricky thing. When I think of my parents getting back together, I remember all of it happening very fast. But when I line up the events that led to it—one domino next to another, I realize that my mother and father got married eight years after he came back into our lives. Eight years of dominoes clicking one against the other and finally crashing spectacularly.

After my mother found me in Nick's bathroom, she broke it off with him. "I had no choice," she said later. "I had to save us—twice."

For years after that, they didn't see each other. It was only when I was hundreds of miles away, and she thought she no longer had to worry about me, that she finally accepted my father's proposal. By then I was twenty-five and had graduated from college. I'd moved to New York City and then to Santa Fe. By then, my grandmother had died. Sometimes I wonder if, had she still been alive, she could have talked my mother out of marrying him again.

My mother didn't look me in the eye when she told me that she knew Nick was an alcoholic but she was marrying him anyway. She stared at the floor and wouldn't own it, as if a force beyond her control pulled the strings. By then he was no longer going on auditions. Because of his alcohol-induced belligerence on television and movie sets, even his longtime agent and actor friends were reluctant to recommend him for parts.

When my parents remarried, I flew back to Los Angeles for their wedding—just a handful of us at the courthouse. Nick was so wasted after the ceremony that he mimed peeing in the set of fancy glasses I'd gotten them as a gift.

Maybe my mother just didn't want to be alone anymore. Maybe she thought marrying him again would make right their original marriage. Maybe she thought it was okay because now that I was gone, he could only hurt her. Or maybe he really was the love of her life, and I never would understand because my father was right—he knew her better than I did.

Part II

Saviors

AUSTIN, TEXAS, WAS A PLACE MY BOYFRIEND WES ALWAYS
went home to. We had been living in Santa Fe for almost two
years when he decided it was time to return once again to his
native city. This time, I went with him.

In Austin, we were staying with his friend Gene. Actually,
with Gene and his wife. From the start, the wife had recognized us as moochers and didn't want us in her guest room.

One morning, Gene quietly asked Wes if we would stay
clear of the house for the evening because he and his wife
were planning to have sex. They were trying to get pregnant,
and he was coming home early because it was a good time of
the month.

That night Wes and I snickered to each other in the car,
which felt good because lately we hadn't been laughing much.

Wes said, "God help us if we ever."

"If we ever what?" I eyed him across the seat.

Without answering, he reached around the wheel, stab-
bing the key into the ignition. He listened to see if the engine
would turn over. With the car safely idling, he looked at me

as if he was still trying to decide, as he had with the car, whether he'd been saddled with a lemon.

While Gene and his wife tried to make a baby, Wes and I wound our way over Hill Country roads. Past the big houses in the grand gated subdivisions that stood in the middle of nowhere, but would one day be surrounded by more of the same—pale creamy buildings with gleaming hardware, over-sized doorways, and circular drives. Wes's lawyer father lived in a house like that. When we came back to Austin, I think we both thought his father might give us such a house. I wondered if that was all it would take to end our troubles. If we had our own house with guest rooms, would we be scheduling sex and making babies?

The road took us beyond the subdivisions to nothing, nothing but rolling hills and darkening lakes. All of a sudden through the car window, one of those breath-catching spots appeared like a painting—a slick of glassy blue beyond smooth white rocks. The kind of view that begs you to stop being you and disappear right into it.

But then Wes ruined it. Squinting one eye shut and pointing to a rocky cove, he talked about swimming there nude with girls as a teenager. I pictured him long-legged and brown, slipping out of his frayed cut-offs with girls who would do that kind of thing—swim naked with boys in the open, their breasts skimming the water, where others might see and judge. I knew that even now I was not such a girl, and knowing that made me pouty and reckless.

Each time the road curved, I looked over the edge and imagined the car flipped like a bug, almost wishing it. But two years before, when I was still living in New York City, if you'd asked me to make a wish, Wes would have been it.

$\sim$

Wes's mother fixed us up. I didn't realize until much later that she did it because she wanted me to fix him up.

Wes was tall and good-looking—a long drink of water. Attractive enough to be disarming but not so pretty as to be intimidating. He was a chef who'd been written up in *The New York Times* as an up-and-comer specializing in the new Southwestern cuisine craze. He was also too smart for his own good, capable of so much and therefore unwilling to do the work mere mortals never question. Admitted to the University of Chicago at sixteen, he'd lasted only a year before he'd gone home to the University of Texas. A few credits shy of his mathematics degree, he dropped out and found his way to cooking.

Just before I met him, he'd been hired to help run a new Santa Fe restaurant that had the culinary world astir. But while he was waiting for the restaurant to open, he ran out of money. People usually stay in a job until the next one starts. But not Wes. That's when he began living in the woods outside Santa Fe, sleeping in a tent, reading books by flashlight, walking into town to wash his hair in the sink of the public library restroom, and hocking his chef's knives for food money. As winter approached and the restaurant and a paycheck were no closer, he'd finally broken down and called his mom for help.

Wes's mother, Isabel, had divorced his lawyer father long ago. A novelist, she'd moved to New York City to live the literary life she'd pined for. She had twelve novels to her name, though I'd never heard of her when I read the 92nd Street Y's brochure for her writing workshop. In the two years since I'd graduated from college, all I'd written were beauty product descriptions, the where-to-buy section, and one sidebar on thigh anxiety for the women's magazine I worked for. I signed up for the workshop to become a real writer.

On the first night, the room was empty when I walked in, except for Isabel sitting on the blackboard side of a large square of desks. Attractive—near sixty, I would find out later, but younger looking—she gazed forward, yogi-like, her folder and books open and ready on the desk. Without speaking, she offered me a bright smile. As the other students arrived, plopping their bags down, scraping their chair legs along the linoleum, Isabel's beatific smile changed to impatient waiting. But whether it was my punctuality or the look of my tailored slacks and sweater—similar to hers—when my turn came to introduce myself, her little smile returned. Silently, we had already agreed: I was her favorite.

In a way, Wes was there that first night too. During the break, Isabel waved a clipping from *The New York Times* at those of us still in the room. She said her chef son, who was the protégé of a celebrity chef out in Santa Fe, had been mentioned by the food critic as someone to watch. During the rest of class, the gray newspaper trailed out the top of her folder, hanging over the edge of her desk.

For each class, I wrote to please Isabel, struggling to strip away the protective coating she said my stories were wrapped in. One night, after I'd volunteered to read a scene I'd written about an out-of-work actor father who looked like the Marlboro Man, she said, "Thank heavens for drunk daddies," with a little laugh as if she'd heard that story before.

I stared straight ahead, tears threatening at her dismissal of my scene as cliché.

A week later, when she returned the finished story to me, she leaned over my shoulder, whispering, "You did it with this one." I saw that she'd scratched out the title I'd chosen, scrawling *Dream Dad* above it. "This could be the start of something bigger," she added.

Walking home that night, bathing myself in thoughts of what that "something bigger" might be, I'd started to cross the street when a taxi honked me back onto the curb. Watching the yellow fender shoot past, I remembered the way Isabel had turned back to me as she stood behind the next student and, with that same strange little smile, said, "I'm glad to see you're a sucker for a cowboy. Growing up in Texas, I've always had that inclination myself."

A few weeks into the class, I'd just gotten home from work when the phone rang. Though Isabel had never called me at home, I recognized her voice instantly when I heard her saying my name on the other end of the line. For all I knew, her purpose could have been mundane—a cancelled class, a change of location—but those reasons for calling did not occur to me. Instead, my heart beat fast.

She didn't go so far as to arrange a date between Wes and me. She simply said her son was flying in from Santa Fe to stay with her for a few days. Then she asked if it would be okay if she gave him my number.

If at first I wondered at the appropriateness of her request, the fact that she'd chosen me turned the infraction into an extension of the complimentary comments she'd left on my work. And so, from the beginning, Wes and my potential as a writer mingled incestuously.

When he called, I liked his Southern accent and the honey in his voice. I wondered what she'd told him about me to make him want to dial my number—had she focused on looks or talent or simply that I was a nice girl? Why did she think meeting me should be a priority during his short visit? He suggested going to a trendy SoHo café that I was not above being impressed by. I told him to look for my long red hair and blue coat. He told me to look for his tall frame and glasses. Not much to go on. But as I walked through the door of the restaurant, he stood, lifting his hand to signal me.

Tall indeed, in loose jeans and an expensive burgundy sweater—the white of his T-shirt filled its cashmere V. Hair, eyes, skin—everything brown. The broad, smooth planes of his face were not what I usually fell for, but there was no denying his appeal. The waitress lingered, scanning him an extra moment while she poured our wine.

Wes had a chef's relish for ordering, and plates of appetizers began crowding our little table. Good-naturedly, he waved the waitress away, saying we'd wait to order the entrées. "We have plenty of time," he said. She shot me an envious little smile.

With his long legs stretching into the aisle, he confessed right away that he'd been married and divorced twice even though he was just shy of thirty. "My mother didn't want me to tell you," he said. "She didn't think you'd like it."

But I did like that he'd told me. He took me in as if my face was the answer to a question he'd been asking for a long time. I already felt important to him.

I called in sick to the magazine, and he stayed with me for the next four days. From my flopped-open futon, as if floating on a raft, I watched him rummaging in my kitchen, a kitchen I used for making coffee and tossing out takeout wrappings. He returned to the stove—jeans hovering at hipbone level, bare chest and feet. Unaware of me, he dipped his little finger into the sauce, tasting and thinking, a gesture that would become familiar. He pushed his glasses into place and turned, aware of me after all, and said with a little grin, "*Puttanesca*. Whore's spaghetti." And because he was never just a cook, but knew things, he said with glee, "Something that could be made in their rooms after sex."

While most young women would not think of their lover's mother at a moment like that, I thought of Isabel. As the days stretched on and her visiting son lingered in my bed rather than catching the train back to her house in White Plains, I wondered if she was pleased. Or did she think her matchmaking had taken hold a little too well?

I had my answer when at the end of the week, on his last night in town, we took the train out to see her because she wanted to cook for us. Not quite ready to look my teacher in the eye, embarrassed by her knowing what we'd been up to, I stood behind Wes on the front step. I focused on the side of his head, the curve of his nice brown ear. Isabel's face suddenly floated next to the ear as she hugged her son. I wondered if he still smelled of our sex. Then she turned to embrace me and I felt the wings of her small shoulder blades. She stepped back with a beaming smile to draw us into her delicious-smelling, oven-warmed house.

By candlelight we feasted on Wes's Texas favorites: pot roast, collard greens in bacon, golden potatoes, Parker House rolls, and chess pie for dessert. We clinked our wine glasses to the success of the match she'd made.

∞

I half expected Wes's interest in me to be a whirlwind fluke. But even before his scent was gone from my pillows, I began receiving long letters urging me not only to visit him in Santa Fe, but to move there, to live with him. Like a soldier writing from the front, he wrote on any paper handy—envelope backs, mismatched stationery, notebook paper with frayed edges. More truths spilled out—about a small trust fund he'd blown, about other universities he'd dropped out of, and always, always about the way he wanted me.

In his mother's class, sometimes it felt as if we were the two people carrying on a romance. We betrayed my fellow students with our knowing glances, her hand on my shoulder, me hanging back after class to go for coffee. Given Wes's history with women, I thought Isabel might have her doubts about the wisdom of me actually considering moving to Santa Fe. But on the last night of the workshop, she indicated I was lucky to have the opportunity at all.

Sliding into our regular booth at the corner coffee shop, she said, "You know, I was going to introduce him to someone else." She named a pretty writer whose first novel I admired. I'd praised the book a few weeks before, but at the time Isabel hadn't said she knew her.

The waiter came over with his green notepad.

"Just coffee," I told him.

"I thought you were having pie?" Isabel seemed genuinely disappointed. But my appetite was gone.

After the waiter left, she said, "This is better, though. You, I mean, not the pie."

I noticed her pink lipstick had traveled to her front teeth, which then disappeared behind her satisfied, close-lipped smile. I suspected then that she hadn't actually planned to introduce Wes to that pretty writer—but she knew that saying she had would make her son even more attractive to me. She thought I would enjoy the idea that I had beaten the other writer. She was right.

When I went home for Christmas a month later, my mother made me blush by buying me a negligee. I sat on the edge of her bed to open the box she'd handed me. She leaned forward for a better look while I shyly lifted the silk nightgown out of its tissue paper. It was pale aqua, a color for a mermaid.

"For your trousseau," she said.

"We're not getting married."

"I want you to feel special."

I'd told her about Wes's letters and the way he had begun insisting that I live with him. I waited for her to warn me not to trust his urgency. For her to say that it had always been the same with my father.

From my fingertips, the silky peignoir hung like a delicate curtain between my mother and me. "What's the worst that can happen?" I asked her. But then I answered my own question, because I thought I knew. After my mother had given birth to me, there'd been no turning back. Once she'd had a child, her life changed forever. "Well, I'm not going to have a baby," I said.

"A baby's not the only thing that can change you," she said.

I had no way to know how living with Wes would change me. I also couldn't know that my being with him would make way for my father to come back into my mother's life yet again.

All I could think at the time, sitting with my mother on her bed, was that I wanted what that peignoir represented. I wanted what was on the other side of the curtain. I was ready to be someone in love. Someone who'd been chosen.

Years later, I would ask my mother why she didn't stop me from moving to Santa Fe with Wes, a decision that derailed a good chunk of my twenties.

"How could I have stopped you?" she said. "I knew you'd already made up your mind. You were going to do what you were going to do. I could only hope that it would be okay."

I wonder now if that is how her parents felt when she first married Nick. When they bought her a beautiful wedding dress and negligees for her trousseau, as if having all the right props would make everything okay.

⌒⌒

Four months after Isabel introduced me to Wes, I quit my magazine job, sold my futon to a friend, packed up my clothes and my cat, and boarded a plane to New Mexico. Wes's chef job had begun by then. He'd rented us a little adobe house with a turquoise door situated at the edge of an *arroyo*, a dry riverbed alive with desert flora and fauna. If we left our patio door open, animals crept in—mice, lizards, and birds. On my first morning there, I saw the thin end of a snake disappear into the bedroom closet among Wes's dark shoes.

In one of his long letters, he had described his ideal scene of love: both of us sitting in the same room and doing our own things, together but not together. From the start, we re-created this scene. Sitting lengthwise on the couch, he at one end and I at the other—our outstretched legs making a yin and yang in the middle. While he read about everything from cooking and poetry to higher mathematics, I tried to write.

Back in New York City, it had sounded good to tell my friends I was going to write a novel, but now that I was in New Mexico, I was easily, willingly distracted—most often drawn to the restaurant where Wes worked. In the beginning, it was that beautiful restaurant—and the sex—that helped me ignore the fact that I'd barely worked on my novel since I'd arrived.

Café Zona was airy with high ceilings and wild Mexican folk art: pink-faced masks, their cupid-bow mouths ready for kissing; coiled psychedelic snakes with playful red velvet tongues; howling coyotes; and Mariachi skeletons wearing spangled sombreros. At one end of the sweeping marble bar, voluptuous stargazer lilies trembled in an enormous vase. At the other end stood icy pitchers of fresh watermelon and mango *licuados* and rows of tall market jars filled with green and red peppers packed in oil.

To go to Zona was like stepping into a dazzling fiesta. Tourists made reservations months in advance, and magazines featured glossy pictures of the food and the art and the gleaming people. The owner was a short, self-important man with a red beard. He wore expensive cowboy boots that clicked with precision on the restaurant's *saltillo* tile floors, pausing only when he stopped to taste from turquoise- and melon-colored plates. Then, the *empresario* had all the time in the world for savoring.

Wes, regal in chef whites, worked the grill. Sitting at the bar and watching him in the exhibition kitchen as he entertained the customers, I anticipated the scent and taste of the smoky mesquite wood lingering on his skin.

After the restaurant closed for the night, the owner would invite Wes and me to sit with him, drinking and trying new dishes, always in one of the big circular pony-skin booths in the back. Watching the two men interact, I always saw an overeagerness in their camaraderie. When one reached to try a smoked duck *empanada* or a lightly battered squash blossom, the other regarded him carefully, Wes pushing his glasses into place, the owner's smile fading into the whiskers of his beard.

One night in particular, they talked about the Yucatán and Oaxaca, where the owner said a woman lived who could teach you the secret of how to make true *mole negro*. I could see Wes bridling under his boss's reins. As I sat between them, watching them laugh at each other's jokes, circling, sizing up one another, I could see Wes asking himself why he didn't already know the secret of *mole*, and why a restaurant like this wasn't his.

"It's you the magazines always want to get a picture of," I would remind him as we lay in bed after evenings at the owner's table. Watching the magnificence of the moon through our window, I would assure him of his greatness and then reach for him to show him that we were in this together. But with no warning, he began to turn away from me. At that point I still didn't understand why things had gone wrong for Wes—the abandoned jobs, the divorces, the college degree left undone—but I knew this was how such problems must have begun.

I was at the restaurant so much that eventually the owner gave me a job. I took reservations and assisted him in his office. I helped him edit his cookbook. I suspected I was also there because Wes and the owner knew I was their peacekeeping ballast.

During the day, as I pretended to write, doodling in my notebook, Wes read more and more. He stacked his books one on top of the other until they toppled into piles by the couch and the bed. When the words didn't come to me, I could have become a reader like him, but between the lines of every book I chose, all I could hear was the writer taunting me for not writing my own.

One afternoon after Wes had already left for the restaurant, I sat at my typewriter and stared at the pale blue keys speckled with liquid paper, and then I called Isabel. "What's the matter with me?" I asked. "In New York it came so much easier. I'm not writing at all anymore." I waited for her to offer one of the stories she had told us in class about her own fits and starts, and perhaps some jumpstart exercise.

But instead she said, "Don't worry about it. This is Wes's time. Not yours."

What about all the potential she'd said she'd seen in me? What about Wes telling me that when his mother first mentioned me to him, she'd talked about how talented I was?

As I sat there feeling sorry for myself, I realized I shouldn't be surprised. She'd conned me all along the way. I was already living in Santa Fe when Wes confessed that his mother had actually sent him a ticket to New York City with the express purpose of introducing him to me. The afternoon before I'd met him, Isabel had taken him to get a haircut. She'd bought him new clothes to spruce him up after his weeks of tent living. She'd given him money to take me out. How many class sessions had it taken for the idea to strike her? That perhaps this neatly dressed young woman with a good job and an affinity for Texas bad boys could save her son.

Had she just gotten tired of rescuing him herself? I'd seen the old prescriptions in the medicine cabinet of our adobe's bathroom, the antidepressants Wes had stopped taking.

With Wes's books scattered at our feet, I began to hate his constant reading. Sitting in a room together but not together, our silent yin and yang made space for me to begin to hate him as well. He must have sensed it; maybe the same thing had happened with his ex-wives. One day he flattened the book he was reading and said accusingly, "What are you looking at?"

I'd been staring over the back of the couch out the window. "I'm just thinking," I said.

"I feel like you're waiting for me to talk to you."

I hauled myself off the couch, sending one of his books spinning across the floor. My bare feet felt the thin layer of desert sand that was always blowing in. I turned to him. "I was just wondering is all. Wondering if the reason your mother chose me for you instead of that novelist is because I'm a bad writer. She must not have wanted to waste a good one on you."

It was the first of our fights that sent me driving off into the night to empty parking lots, where I sat and waited to cool off. Fights that brought him close to my face, when I could see his fists clenching and unclenching next to his sides. Now I was the one who turned away in bed, but instead of leaving me alone as he had for months, my indifference sparked aggression. I'd wake in the night and find him on top of me with little concern for what I wanted, taking my clothes off with the same insistence he'd had about wanting me to move in with him. Sometimes I submitted timidly, victimized. Sometimes I responded fiercely as if, through sex, I could get back at him for everything that was wrong about us.

Wes held on to his sous chef job at Zona for nearly two years. And then came Austin, and Gene and Gene's wife. The day we arrived at their house, we sat in their living room, drinking iced tea as Wes wove expensive talk about the restaurant he planned to open in Austin. He was convinced his father would front him the money. Gene's wife looked dubious. To defy her tightly crossed arms and permed curls, I spent days at their kitchen table being a dutiful girlfriend by making appointments with commercial real estate agents. We began to tour restaurants whose bad locations had led to several changes in ownership until, finally, they stood empty.

As Wes and I wandered the echoing kitchens and dining rooms, playing restaurateurs, I sometimes thought I heard the fast, haughty steps of Zona's owner back in Santa Fe. Then I would slip my hand into Wes's and hold on. The tightness with which he was ready to squeeze back always surprised me. At times like that, I wanted to shake Gene's skinny-shouldered wife. I wanted to ask her who she thought she was, judging us—tell her that Wes and I were the kind of people for whom greatness was an option. I wanted to take her back to New York City for proof, back to where each of us had once shone with promise.

At other times, I saw it exactly her way. When Wes and I were in a coffee shop with mirrored walls, I'd catch our reflection. Then I could see how my once stylish haircut, long and glossy, had disappeared, as overgrown as an old hedge. In a photo booth strip of black and white photos, I saw my skin like dust, Wes's cheekbones fading into a binge drinker's puffiness, our eyes looking out as dull and flat as our hopes.

The night Gene and his wife were trying to get pregnant, Wes and I drove and drove past those cliff edges until we were driving in the dark and the hills were inky cutouts against the sky. And then we went to a bar so we could feel that we were part of the world once again.

We drank martinis with big green olives, magnified in elegantly tapered glasses so they looked even fatter at the bottom of icy gin. After four of them, I said I was going to the ladies' room. Instead, I poured change into a pay phone, trying to keep my balance as I leaned against a wall.

As soon as I heard my father's voice, glad it was he who had answered and not my mother, I started sobbing in great gulps. "I'm coming to get you," he said.

I pictured him with his ear to the phone, thrilled to be the parent called to duty rather than my mother. I knew if I gave him the signal, he would fasten the big western belt buckle that always hung heavily from his jeans, undone until the last moment. Then, weathered and wrung out, he would slide behind the wheel of his souped-up Ford Ranger and drive through the night to rescue me. Because that's what people did in my family—they saved each other even though they were always falling apart themselves.

"No. No. Don't come here," I said in the middle of my drunken crying jag. He got scared then because he'd never heard me like this. "I'm going to get your mom," he said.

"No, don't. Don't get her. I'm okay." But of course he was right. In the end it would be my mother who would come for me. She would arrive weeks later and we would pack up what little I had left and I would go back to Los Angeles to start a new life. I would pick up my battle with my father all over again when I got there. But I would never forget how he'd wanted to drive through the night to save me.

Wes and I were among the last people to leave the bar. Back in Gene's guest room, I stripped off my sweater and pants, slipping quickly under the covers, not wanting Wes to see me. When I woke again, the room was yellow with the late afternoon sun, and I knew I had slept through most of the day. Wes was there beside me, awake too. Seeing me stir, he moved in closer.

At the touch of his bare brown legs on mine, I felt the resentment I often did when he wanted to take what he thought was his. But now, at last, I knew that we were over and that soon I would move on, and that made me feel impulsive and wild—the way I had felt while looking over the cliff's edge the night before. Something forbidden charged my skin. Aroused, I began to move under him.

Lost in the sound of our breathing, we didn't hear the car drive up, the keys jangle in the door. We heard nothing until someone in the living room blasted the stereo to drown out what we were doing. We froze, staring at each other, realizing we'd been discovered.

Wes's brown eyes, always a bit like a stranger's to me when he wasn't wearing his glasses, flitted slightly from side to side as they tried to take in my whole face at once. Then his pretty lips broke into a wolfish smile, revealing white, white teeth. We pressed our noses into each other's shoulders, feeling the soft shaking of our laughter, relieved for the moment to smile like children at our own naughtiness, willing to believe for a little while longer that we might still save one another.

Makeshift
Twins

LIVING IN A BUBBLE OF TWO HAD ALWAYS FELT NATURAL to me. How often, while growing up, I had heard my mother say, "Just we two." She'd squeeze my hand, smiling in camaraderie. It wasn't until many years after I'd been out on my own that I realized I expected such camaraderie from others. Not knowing any other way, I'd been re-creating that close one-to-one dynamic in my friendships beginning in elementary school and continuing on through adulthood. Never more so than with Liz.

We met on move-in day during our freshman year at a small college in Southern California—a gem of Spanish-style architecture with manicured lawns, hidden courtyards, and gently bubbling fountains. Liz was from Boston, where she'd been the president of her senior class and a champion on the ski and debate teams. Her beauty had caught the eye of a talent scout and she'd acted in a few television commercials that were now helping to pay her tuition. When I told her my goal was to move to New York City after college to become a magazine editor and write novels, she said, "Me, too!"

Later, Liz would confess that when I'd introduced myself, her breath caught in her throat—she was sure I was about to say my name was Annabelle, a character in the Rona Jaffe novel *Class Reunion* about lifelong friends who meet in college. She'd been obsessed with the novel all summer. As she confided this, she pulled the book from her shelf, showing me the cover illustration. Annabelle had shoulder-length auburn hair like mine. Further proof that Liz and I were destined to become best friends.

Like me, Liz had grown up with a single mother. Yet our maternal crucibles had forged me one way and her, another. I'd stayed tentative, forever pacing the sidelines of a grown-up world and yearning to jump in. Liz dove into the deep end on a regular basis.

On the first night of orientation, the guys from a neighboring dorm stormed our hallways, banging on doors and dragging girls from their rooms. I hid in my closet, convinced gang rapes were about to take place. After the whooping and shrieking died down, I emerged to find a group of flannel-nightgowned women peering into the courtyard below. On an improvised stage, there was Liz in pajama top and panties linking arms with a row of girls doing a Rockettes kick line while fifty guys serenaded them. I was in awe of her ease. While I'd hidden, she'd known just what to do. But the next day, she confided that she was just as embarrassed as I was, because she'd gone along and given them what they wanted.

Liz was as drawn to me as I was to her. She saw past my shyness that others often mistook for conceit. In a college town full of Saabs and BMWs, she didn't judge me because I wasn't a debutante who summered on Martha's Vineyard the way she did. And when she ran across the dorm hallway into my room and asked me to drive her to a pharmacy for the morning-after pill, I didn't judge her either. My virginity had become a burden I was all too ready to unload. "I didn't want to shock you," she said after telling me she'd slept with the cute senior we'd met at a party the night before. She waited for him to call but he never did, the first of many men I saw take advantage of her.

Among my new friends, Liz was the only one I trusted enough to take home with me—to see the modest way in which my mother and I lived. No doorman building. Just a two-bedroom apartment with a carport in back. She was fascinated by my mother—a woman on her own who hadn't gone to college but had read every book on our floor-to-ceiling bookshelves and saved enough for us to travel to Europe many times.

After I met Liz's mother, I understood why she admired the capability of mine.

Grace came to town one weekend to see Liz in a play. In slacks and turtleneck, she had the slim, athletic build of a tennis player and that old-fashioned, upper-class accent you hear in Katharine Hepburn movies. Her big brown eyes and apple cheeks were just like Liz's, but behind those eyes was someone playing along until she could get in on the joke. I wondered if her blankness was why Liz's father, a civil rights lawyer, had left her. Or if his divorcing her was the cause.

I knew my mother leaving Nick when I was a baby had been for the best. But Liz felt the wrongness of her father's absence like the ache of a phantom limb. Late at night in the dorm, she spoke of her summers on Martha's Vineyard with her father's family the way an exile might speak of her home country. Only on the island did she feel whole again.

⌒

Even though we looked nothing alike—Liz was tall and honey-skinned, lithe with delicate bones, and I was fair, petite, and curvy—people started remarking on a resemblance between us. Our mannerisms, speech patterns, and clothing styles had blended. "*Les Deux Femmes*," people called us when we took a French class together. "Where's your other half?" they asked when one of us was spotted alone.

We began to share everything from makeup to diaphragm jelly (once I did lose my virginity to a popular but forgettable boy). We started an alternative campus newspaper together and cohosted a radio show. She celebrated Thanksgiving and Easter with my mother and me. I spent the summer with her on Martha's Vineyard doing all the things she'd told me about—beach bonfires, blueberry picking, and milkshakes at the golf club.

During sophomore year, Liz fell deeply, almost violently, in love with our English professor. He was young, unmarried, and his classes filled up fast. He spotted her in the third row of Modern American Lit and asked her to lunch one day when I wasn't in class. Not long after, he asked her to bed. As her best friend, I was in on their secret affair, which stretched into our junior year abroad in Paris, where he was on sabbatical, and continued once we returned to campus.

One day senior year, I ran into the professor. He was turning down the path to his house when he saw me and asked if I'd take a couple of books to Liz. I stood just inside his open door as he rummaged around a dining table piled high with books and papers.

"Ah," he said, plucking the volumes from a stack. With his beaming smile, he walked toward me—books in his outstretched arm, shirtsleeves rolled, forearm flexing—and, as if it was the most natural thing in the world, kissed me. When I didn't kiss him back, he straightened and retreated to the dining room. For an instant I thought I'd imagined it. But as I met his eyes I knew he was already wondering if I would tell Liz—and I knew I never would. I couldn't risk our friendship by hurting her.

In the end, Liz found out on her own that he couldn't be trusted. One day, when he was in class and she was lingering at his house, she noticed a diary on his desk—a Pandora's box she couldn't resist. In explicit sexual detail, he'd chronicled encounters he'd had with her and another student on the same day. He referenced each girl by hair color—"the sexy blonde," "the luscious brunette." I still wonder sometimes if he kissed me simply to add a redhead to his collection.

Even after she knew of his infidelity, I kept the professor's kiss a secret because I'd admitted to myself that part of me had liked it. Not because I wanted him, but because he'd wanted me.

A rivalry with Liz had begun to burn in me. I weighed my looks and talents against hers the way I had compared myself to my mother when I was growing up. The attention of others was my barometer. I looked for proof that people thought I was more than Liz's sidekick. That kiss had proved it.

Intellectually, I knew better. But I was like a needy dog nudging its head under your elbow after another dog gets a pat. It galled me to recognize in myself the same pining that had driven my father to swim darkly in his alcoholic brew as others "made it" and he didn't. Vanity, selfishness, envy, insecurity—his worst traits woven together, slithering here and there, whipping a serpentine tail across my gut and into my heart.

After graduation, Liz and I did go off to New York City to become magazine editors—or more accurately, lowly editorial assistants—at competing women's magazines. Plucked from among scores of applicants, we were grateful to land these coveted spots. It was the mid-'80s, when bright young things ruled publishing. A literary "brat pack" included Bret Easton Ellis, Tama Janowitz, and Jay McInerney, with twenty-something editors launching both *Spy* and *Sassy* magazines. People rose up the food chain fast. As I read through the slush pile and edited relationship columns, success seemed inevitable, like something you waited in line for until they called your name.

Then Liz's name did get called, and she was promoted.

Whereas I had been a model assistant—my boss referring to me as the perfect protégé in a talk to young publishing hopefuls—I now champed at the bit for a better title. No longer content to be a good little helper, my hunger for recognition became my downfall.

On the day I got fired, the editor-in-chief called me into her office. "In the future, if you want to advance, you would do well to think more about making your boss look good," she said. I learned the *Seventeen* editor I'd asked about a job had called my boss to report my disloyalty. Taking the Lexington Avenue bus home that day, I was convinced the other riders could see my scarlet "F"—fired, failure, father's daughter.

Like any good friend, Liz blamed my bosses, not me. I found a new job soon enough—one with the title I'd been seeking. But getting fired had shaken me. Without admitting it to myself, I'd already begun looking for a face saving exit from New York City. Then I found one. His name was Wes.

I don't remember what Liz said when I told her I was moving to Santa Fe with a handsome chef. I don't remember if she tried to stop me, questioned the impulsiveness of my decision. Or if she felt relieved to get some distance between "*Les Deux Femmes.*" If she was aware of the burning competition I felt with her—if she had ever felt it too—she never said. I think we both thought that acknowledging any jealousy between us could end our friendship.

After I moved, Liz and I kept up by phone. Close to two years later, she visited me in Santa Fe. By then, Wes had lost his job at Café Zona and was working shifts at the Hilton. Scanning the bare hangers in my closet, Liz asked, "Where are all your clothes?"

I didn't know where they were. Maybe when Wes and I had moved from the adobe house to a cheaper apartment, a box of my jeans and T-shirts had gotten lost along the way. Maybe I'd left the better stuff at a consignment store the way I'd pawned my jewelry, because we needed money to pay rent. Like every part of my life since I'd left New York City—from my now meager book collection to my limp, falling-out hair—my wardrobe had devolved to dregs.

Too far gone to keep up a good front, I finally confessed to Liz that the moment the plane had touched down in New Mexico, I knew I'd made a mistake moving there. Wes wasn't a mean drunk like my father; he was a depressive one who spiraled into silent broods and refused to refill his lithium prescription. As for my career, I'd written a few freelance articles for editor friends back in New York City, but I hadn't touched my novel.

"You've got to get out of here," she said when she hugged me good-bye at the airport. "Leave," she whispered in my ear.

Being with Liz was like seeing my old self again. The shock of how far my life had veered off the course I'd set for myself in college—a path she was still on—ultimately helped convince me to leave Wes and reboot my life. The next year my mother rescued me from Austin and brought me back to Los Angeles, and I started a new job as an editor with a non-profit organization.

Free again, whizzing along Mulholland Drive, sunroof open, Talking Heads blaring on the radio, I told myself I'd never lose control of my life like that again.

◦⁀◦

Liz and I were on the brink of turning thirty when she called to tell me her boyfriend had given her an engagement ring. I'd been in L.A. for a couple of years by then. Bracing myself in the doorway of my kitchen the way I'd done when the last earthquake struck, I matched her excited shrieks with my own—even as I thought, *Oh god, oh god, I'm being left behind.* In that moment, I understood my competition with Liz had never been about a desire to best her, but rather my fear of being stranded as she moved on, unable to progress to my own happy ending.

The following summer, I watched her marry on the lawn of her grandmother's house on Martha's Vineyard, the ocean glittering in the distance. Her aunts teased me when I made my toast because I could barely get the words out through tears. Perhaps I didn't have the right to feel the moment so deeply. I wasn't family. But even as I worried I would never have what Liz had—family and friends gathered together to watch me marry a man I loved—her dazzling vitality pierced me in a way I would not feel again until years later when I was a mother. Standing at the edge of a competition ring, watching my audacious daughter on the cusp of adolescence—wild, berry-lipped, with legs as long and coltish as the horse she rode, so ready to seize all that the world held for her—I would flash on Liz's blinding beauty and remember how my heart had swelled on her wedding day.

❧

While I had no inkling at her wedding that my luck with men was about to change, Liz did. I'd told her about the men

I'd been dating—a lawyer and a Bank of America executive. She had a smile in her voice when she said, "I like the other one. The one you're 'just friends' with."

I'd mentioned to her a lanky, blue-eyed guy named Brad whom I'd met while volunteering on a political campaign. Liz sensed from the start that he was the one, and she was right. In the fall of 1992, a little more than a year after she'd married, I had a wedding of my own.

For a time after that, Liz and I seemed to be on the same path again. Like a sledder on a hill, she had always thrown her Flexible Flyer down first, gliding smoothly on her way. I'd been the one to follow, flopping on my belly, unsure of the terrain. Now it seemed we'd both gotten to that safe place we'd longed for since we first met in college—a life where we'd mended the mistakes of our parents, where we were loved and whole. Miraculously, my false start with Wes had not mattered. *Olly olly oxen free,* I wanted to cheer.

Yet even at my wedding, if I'd been paying attention, I would have noticed that Liz and I were actually on different sledding hills altogether. Despite the charming photo my wedding photographer took of Liz sitting in her husband's lap at the reception, I'd found her later that night crying in the bathroom. She had the scared face of a child startled from a bad dream. "I'm okay. Don't worry," she kept saying, not wanting to spoil my day. Later I realized that my wedding had sparked in her the same mix of happiness for a friend and anxiety over her own fate that her wedding had once stirred in me.

A few weeks after that, she called to say she couldn't stop

thinking about a sexy writer she'd met. "Maybe I should just sleep with him and get it over with," she said, as if her infidelity was inevitable.

I'd never judged her before, but this time I felt myself recoil. "There's no going back from that," I said.

Through the receiver, I heard her exhale. "You're right," she said, as if I'd kept her from plunging into the deep end just in time.

⌁

Shortly after Liz had her first child, I traveled to New York City for a conference. Rather than staying in a hotel, I slept on her couch. Imposing on a couple with a newborn probably wasn't the best idea, but I was still operating the way we always had, taking any chance to be together.

I'd reserved the last day of my trip just for Liz and me—carving out the morning to replay our old single days of scouring vintage shops and hanging out at the Columbus Bakery. What I wanted for our morning was a glorious fall day—the kind only New York City can unfurl before you. What we got was gloom and gray. What I wanted was our old simpatico, each of us adding another building block to the conversation until it towered and toppled and we started a new one. Instead, we walked in silence, her son in a Baby Björn like a star on her chest, his tiny arms and legs dangling. When we'd embarked on our day together, we'd left behind dirty dishes piled high in her sink and hardwood floors in desperate need of a sweep. We'd also left behind her husband sitting on the couch, pretending to read the newspaper.

For days, I'd tried not to hear them arguing down the hall. I didn't acknowledge how unnerved I'd been by her husband screaming at their crying baby, and Liz screaming back at him to stop it. Their fights had been a train wreck out in the open, cars mangled, casualties moaning. I doubt she would have let anyone but me see them like that.

As rain began to fall, we agreed to skip shopping and head straight to the bakery. Espresso machine hissing, muffins piled high in the case before us, Liz whispered, "I've got to nurse him again," and took off to find a table.

Trying not to slosh our coffees, I spotted her in a corner, Baby Björn unsnapped, shirt lifted. She watched me make my way over to her. Did she feel the same rising panic I did? I tried not to meet her eyes, not wanting to say what I felt sure we were both thinking.

As if she'd read my mind, she said, "I feel like I married the wrong guy." She dropped a sugar cube in her cup. "I feel like I married someone who should be on my list of former boyfriends, instead of waiting for *the one* the way you did."

Admitting this out loud made it real. We knew this conversation could take her down a path we both dreaded: the unraveling of a marriage, separation, divorce, a woman raising children by herself—fears we'd shared with each other back in our college dorm rooms.

I imagined the life Liz and her baby might have on their own. She would be capable and stoic like my mother. But I couldn't help thinking about the early days of my childhood:

the way the lights used to go out when my mother couldn't pay the electric bill, and how sometimes we'd need to search our pockets in hopes of finding grocery money. I remembered that first apartment in L.A., and the alley in back where I'd been molested after school. How hard my mother had worked to protect me, but sometimes she just couldn't. How I'd always been aware that it was just we two, with no one else to help us. This was not the life I wanted for my friend and her son.

I tried to concentrate on the cheeriness of the café, not the bleakness of her situation. But Liz must have seen pity in my eyes. Is that what made her reach for my wrist to check my watch? I had plenty of time before my flight, but she said, "We'd better get back. You have to go and he'll be wondering where I am." As I followed her out of the café, I kept to myself the news I'd been waiting to share with her: My baby daughter was already growing inside me.

Out on the street, she stuck a hand in the air to hail a cab. A scrum of yellow taxis raced toward us, the victorious driver lurching to the curb. Liz cupped her baby's feet as she slid along the black vinyl seat after me. She called out her address and the cabbie tsked as he pulled away. It was the kind of short, low-fare trip cab drivers hate.

We'd barely come to a stop at her apartment when she stuck a twenty-dollar bill through the plastic window, saying, "You got the food. I'll pay for the cab." It was a point of pride. Her marriage might be falling apart, but she could manage cab fare.

That's when the driver said, "No."

"Excuse me?" Liz said.

"Need small," he grunted.

I reached into my purse. "It's okay. I've got it."

"No," she shushed me. "He can make change."

I caught the cabbie's eyes in the rearview mirror. I realized English wasn't his native language. He must have understood just enough to get the drift of our conversation, but he'd misinterpreted, thinking we were making his life difficult just because we could. He turned around in his seat, one arm hugging the wheel. "You play with me?" He glared. "Get out."

"Liz, I've got it," I said, but she didn't want my help. She shrugged at the driver as if to say, "Whatever, your loss." She put the twenty back in her wallet and we scooted across the seat, Liz cradling her son.

I thought the driver would peel off in a rage—caring less about the low fare than having to shell out all his small bills for change—but he opened his door and climbed out. He was young and big. His short-sleeved shirt strained to contain his biceps and chest. "Stupid women," he said, towering over us.

"Here," I said, holding out money. Instead of taking it, he spit on the ground in disgust. Scared now and just wanting to get away from him, Liz and I hurried up the front steps of her apartment building.

He followed.

She began to pat her pockets, and I knew she'd forgotten her keys. The cabbie stood behind us, shifting on the balls of his feet like a boxer. He puffed up his chest, directing his anger first at Liz, then at me. "I know where you live," he said.

Liz banged on the front door. We could see her building super through the glass. "Let us in," she called to him, but he didn't want to open the door because of the yelling driver. "Please," she said. "I've got my baby." Finally, the super opened the door. Liz with her little son slipped through.

Why I pressed my luck I'm not sure, but after catching the open door I turned back to the cabbie and said, "We weren't playing with you." This time he drew back and spit directly in my face. "I know where you live," he said again.

Wiping his spittle from my nose and cheeks with my sleeve, I hurried through the door, pushing it closed behind me. Liz stood by the elevator, her cheek pressed to the top of her son's head, barely registering that I'd made it inside safely.

As we rode up in the elevator, I continued wiping my face on my sleeve. The driver's words lingered: *I know where you live.* Yet he had no idea. Liz knew it and so did I. For years, we'd been fashioning ourselves into makeshift twins but this was her life, and I was going home.

When we'd first met, we were two daughters abandoned in different ways by our fathers and longing to be loved. We recognized in one another a determination not to repeat the mistakes of our mothers. Mistakes that had left Liz feeling the phantom limb of her missing father and me the slithering envy and insecurity of mine. I had always thought that of the two of us, Liz would be the one to reach safe harbor. Yet now I found myself on dry land, watching the undertow clutch at her. I was unable to pull her to safety the way she had done for me when she told me to leave Wes. *Stay. Leave.* I didn't know what advice to give her. I only knew that once again, she was moving ahead of me in life experience. This time, I had no intention of following her.

For years after the taxi incident, after Liz had another baby and I had two, I still hoped our destiny was to be life-long friends. Even though it now took her days to return my calls, and sometimes she never did. Still, when I was in New York City I made it a point to get together with her. During one of those trips she told me she was getting a divorce. She'd been dealing with it for over a year. It stunned me to learn I was the last to know.

I understood then that she had divorced me long ago, sitting across from each other in the Columbus Bakery on that gloomy gray day. Scared about her marriage, stroking her baby's velvety head, she must have seen my relief. She must have seen how very glad I was, at last, to be me and not her. Perhaps she'd even heard my heart calling out, *Olly olly oxen free.*

The
Proposal

OUR CHILDREN OFTEN ASK THEIR FATHER AND ME TO
tell them stories about our life together before they were
born. They like hearing how Brad confessed that he was "ro-
mantically inclined" toward me when we were supposed to be
just friends. They're intrigued by the way we made up our
own wedding ceremony, including a question-and-answer
session with our guests that mimicked the political events we
attended during that phase in our lives. But the story of our
marriage proposal is not one we often tell, especially to our
kids. Within it lurks a clue it took me years to decipher.
Some people might even read our proposal story as a warning
that we should not have married at all.

We met while making get-out-the-vote calls for an as-
piring California state assemblyman. At the candidate's
headquarters, Brad and I were designated leaders of a pod of
volunteers heading to a nearby phone center. We all piled
into my Volkswagen, and Brad rode shotgun. Strangers that
first night, we were pressed close in the capsule of my tiny
car. Our breath charged with the excitement of election night

and political action, my skirt riding up my thigh as I worked the stick from first to fifth.

I learned that as a UC Berkeley student he'd had purple hair and frequented mosh pits. He'd only been out of school for a couple of years, trading in his punk lifestyle for suits and a fundraising job with the University of California in Los Angeles. Actually, only one suit—a single-breasted navy pinstripe that he wore every day. It showed off his height and broad shoulders.

At the time, I worked for a nonprofit called Town Hall in downtown Los Angeles—a forum that hosted dignitaries like Jimmy Carter, Benazir Bhutto, and Mikhail Gorbachev. Unbeknownst to me, my husband-to-be referred to me as "the Town Hall babe" to his colleagues. I'd never thought of myself as a *babe*, but had always hoped to inspire such admiration.

In the beginning, our love for the City of Angels and our burgeoning love for each other were entwined. He became part of a young Los Angeles leaders group I'd formed through my office. We worked at a food bank together and helped rebuild distressed neighborhoods after the Rodney King riots. We went door-to-door for political candidates and attended civic meetings on topics ranging from police reform to public transportation and homelessness. Even though we weren't dating, we made excuses to meet up—free event tickets or a mutual friend's birthday party, often at city landmarks like Griffith Park Observatory, the La Brea Tar Pits, and Venice Beach.

We finally went on an official date when the event we

were supposed to attend was cancelled and he casually asked if I wanted to get together anyway. That was my first confirmation that he liked me as much as I secretly liked him. Our Friday-night dinner turned into breakfast the next morning. Saturday biking in the Santa Monica Mountains turned into slow dancing in his living room that night, which led to Sunday brunch and the late show of *Blade Runner* at the Rialto. Sunday night led us to Monday morning carpooling to work. We moved in together shortly thereafter.

Unlike when I'd moved across the country to live with Wes, I never had any qualms about my decision to be with Brad. From the start everything was easy with him. I kept waiting for the moment of awkwardness I'd had at the beginning of every previous relationship—when we both would realize we'd had enough of the closeness for a while and needed our own space. With Brad that moment never came.

The night he proposed, we were having dinner at one of our favorite restaurants, a kitschy Italian place on Vermont where the waiters sang opera and served thin-crust pizza on tall table stands. We were sitting in a red leather booth when he turned to me and said the very words: "Will you marry me?"

It's all happening, I thought. Those words I'd anticipated all my life. "Yes, yes," I said. "Of course. I love you. Yes." Afterward, we went to the Dresden Room—a lounge next door—to toast our future over Manhattans, clinking the rims of our glasses before we sipped.

But five months later, while talking with friends about our impending nuptials, he denied he'd been the one to say the words. He said I asked him. Our friends changed the subject. Like a needle scratching across a record, the evening came to an abrupt halt.

Perhaps because everything between us had been so easy up to that point, we were able to quickly put aside this disagreement over who asked whom. Perhaps because we were so in sync about everything else, it didn't seem to matter in the grand scheme of our relationship. The proposal became like a spill of red wine on new carpet, gasp-worthy in the moment, then a fading stain you winced at only when you made yourself notice.

We planned to go to Paris for our honeymoon. We chose rings, a cake, and a wedding meal to serve to family and friends. Along with nine other couples, we went to a Making Marriage Work class that was like a version of *The Newlywed Game*. At one point, we were asked to switch partners and converse with the opposite-sex member of another couple. "Notice your increased heart rate with a stranger," our teacher instructed us. "Your quickening pulse, the flirtation, the intrigue, the pressure to seduce. That's how it was when you first met your partner, right? Remember what that felt like. Keep it alive between you throughout your marriage."

Listening to the other couples in class, we counted ourselves lucky that we didn't have the kind of meddling parents they described. Ours were happy to leave us to our own devices. They gave us money—an equal share from each—to do what we wanted for the wedding.

By then, my mother had walked out on Nick for the second time. His raging and violence had driven her to keep a "go bag" in her car. One night instead of checking into a hotel again, she sublet a new apartment. He finally agreed to divorce her on the condition that she continued supporting him. I didn't even tell Nick about the wedding for fear he'd show up drunk.

Our class teacher, a marriage therapist, told us that sex, money, and disagreeing on big issues (such as having children) before the wedding were always the underlying causes of broken marriages. Brad and I thought we had our bases covered. Wanting kids was something we'd talked about early. As for money, we'd already opened a joint bank account and pooled our resources. And when the teacher read (anonymously) everyone's answers to the question of how many times we wanted sex each week, I just knew that we were the two who'd given the highest numbers. We took satisfaction in knowing that if we'd been playing *The Newlywed Game* for real, we'd be winning.

On a sunny September morning, we married. Making our entrance to the ceremony at the same time, we descended opposite marble staircases in a historic building in the heart of downtown L.A. I wore a dress made of vintage French lace. The political candidate we'd volunteered for officiated the ceremony. We had a wedding lunch on the deck of a low-key but trendy restaurant off Vine Street in Hollywood. Instead of rice, our friends tossed environmentally-friendly birdseed, and they gave us a pair of new mountain bikes festooned with bows.

When we arrived at the Chateau Marmont—an L.A. icon where we planned to stay for our first night of marriage—it felt more like a grandmother's dowdy guest room than the elegant suite we'd envisioned. The bellhop had just left. Champagne was on its way. Fully clothed, we lay back on the chenille bedspread. We turned to each other, our faces on the bed, and made our first important decision as a married couple.

"Let's leave," we said in unison. We practically skipped out the hotel door, checking into the Bel Age on Sunset instead. In plushy bathrobes the next morning, enjoying breakfast on the balcony overlooking the city, we congratulated ourselves for not settling. We were elated that we'd found each other and that we each knew the other's heart and mind so well.

～

Five days short of our first wedding anniversary, I went to bed early. I had a big day at work the next morning—alarm clock set, my suit, shoes, and jewelry laid out. After bending down to kiss my husband good night, I left him in the living room watching television.

Hours later, I woke with the moon shining gray-blue through the curtains. He was beside me, then over me, his randy mood obvious. He didn't know that in that moment, he reminded me of Wes—and the salty guilt I'd sometimes felt when I would wake to find Wes taking off my clothes and then go along with it just to keep the peace.

Brad also didn't know how relieved I was that, in the dark of our room that night, I wasn't afraid the way I sometimes was with Wes. I could tell my husband that I needed to sleep, and he would still love me. When Brad heard "no" that night, he simply went to sleep, and so did I.

The next morning, when we were standing in the kitchen dressed and ready to go our separate ways, I said, "I didn't know who you were last night."

In his starched white shirt and navy tie, he looked at me, startled. He'd been about to take a sip of coffee but stopped. "Why, what do you mean?"

"It was just kind of weird," I said. "You knew I had to get up early to get ready for my meeting."

Through gold-rimmed glasses that always struck me as a Clark Kent disguise, his blue eyes searched me. He didn't reveal it then, with me on my way out the door, but he had no idea what I was talking about.

After work that evening, we sat on our Sven couch from IKEA as he told me his version of what had happened the night before.

He had no recollection of coming to our room. He didn't remember waking me. He didn't remember me pushing him away or telling him "no." Apparently that morning had been like many other mornings we'd shared: him asking me questions, gathering intel, trying to piece together the previous night's blackout. Only this time, I'd said something that scared him: *I didn't know who you were.*

He revealed that he'd thought it would be different with me. That from that first weekend we'd spent together, I'd become the talisman he held up to an addiction he'd been hiding since he was fifteen. He told me that after I went to bed, he finished the wine we'd opened at dinner and then he finished another bottle. And then he wasn't himself. And for the first time, I saw him that way.

As he spoke, I looked at our wedding picture on a nearby shelf. I stared at my stupid smiling face, the French lace of my dress, and the bouquet of gardenias as I took in the fact that I'd been fooled. I didn't really know my husband at all. How had I ignored the clues? Why hadn't I noticed all of the morning interrogations as he tried to reconstruct the activities of the night before?

Or had I?

At the bar we frequented, hadn't I recently taken to downing his third bourbon with all its "tobacco, woody, smoky" bullshit that he and the bartender discussed in loving detail? Wasn't that the same thing as pouring my father's booze down the drain the way my mother and I had? Had I intuited that three bourbons after sharing a bottle of wine with me was a line my husband shouldn't cross?

It was like a preposterous Greek tragedy. At the beginning of the story, the oracle predicts an outlandish outcome and you wonder how it could happen—no one would intentionally kill his father and marry his mother. No child of an alcoholic would intentionally choose one as the father of her children. But just like in *Oedipus Rex,* the improbable came true. My husband didn't act like any of the other drunks I'd known. He didn't rage. He wasn't depressed. He didn't sabotage good jobs and he'd never been in jail.

It was only then that I understood why his memory of proposing to me had been lost in a blur. A shared moment I'd filled with so much meaning—a moment I assumed we both brought to every experience of "us"—wasn't shared at all.

A few days later, we celebrated our anniversary in a French bistro without wine and with little conversation. He'd been to five Alcoholics Anonymous meetings—one every day. At the time, I didn't know how lucky I was. I didn't know that a single event—his coming to me like that in the night, and my calling him on what he'd done the next day, something I'd never done with any man before—would change our lives for the better forever.

Because in the immediate aftermath, I was angry in a way I didn't know how to handle. Feeling more betrayed than I ever had, I stewed and sulked. To me, alcoholics were people who repeatedly, inevitably disappointed you. They said sorry all the time for things they did again and again. Alcoholics were people who claimed they loved you but in the end they left you or you had to leave them. I just wanted Brad to say it had all been a mistake. That he wasn't an alcoholic after all.

For months while he went to meetings, I stayed home. He told me I should go to Al-Anon. I was not in the habit of swearing, but I screamed back at him, "Don't fucking tell me about Al-Anon!" I told him I'd known about the group for "family and friends of alcoholics" long before he did. When I'd first moved back to L.A., I'd gone to a few meetings, sharing about my father, about Wes, about my grandmother who'd died prematurely from the disease, and about my Uncle Don, who by the time I was in junior high had taken to sobbing on my shoulder about his life's regrets. I thought I'd escaped all that when I found Brad.

But finally, after sitting home alone night after night, I did go to Al-Anon with an "I'll show you" hostility. Ninety meetings in ninety days was what they told AA newbies. If he could do it, so could I.

One Saturday near the ninety-day mark, I was driving home from a meeting, stuck in traffic on the 101 Freeway. I glanced at my Al-Anon books lying on the seat beside me. So far, all the stories I'd heard had been about dealing with the kinds of addicts I'd known before—mean, scheming, unreliable, maudlin, itinerant. That was not my husband. As I waited for the car in front of me to move, I picked up one of the books and began thumbing through it. The phrase "suffocating grip of self-pity" jumped out at me.

The woman in the story had come to Al-Anon when her husband was already sober. Rather than fearing his drinking, she feared him seeking solutions without her. She feared him getting well while her own soul festered. Would he get better and leave her?

I thought about the self-pity I'd wallowed in for the last few months because our happily ever after wasn't turning out the way I'd planned. Since my earliest childhood memories, I'd never really been at home in my own skin. Like the woman in the story, I had always looked to others to feel happy and whole— relying on my mother to soothe every wound, on my father to be my "dream dad," on Liz to love me like a sister. On romantic partners to love me as unconditionally as my mother always had. And when I found the man I wanted to spend the rest of my life with and who wanted to spend his life with me, I thought I was home free. But none of it turned out to be enough.

While I was lost in thought, I didn't notice my foot lifting from the brake. The front of my car nudged up to the car ahead, pushing repeatedly at its bumper. The other driver craned his head around. We looked at each other in anger and confusion. For a panicked moment, I didn't know how to stop the bumping and pushing. I'd forgotten how to operate the car. Finally I stepped on the brake as if I'd only just discovered its purpose.

I clung to the steering wheel. Nearly all my life a refrain had wafted through my head like a line from a poem or a song or a cry to my mother: *I want to go home* it sang to me, even when I was home. It rose up in me even when I was with those I loved most. It rose up in me now.

After that, I started going to meetings for no one but me.

❧

We hadn't talked about the marriage proposal in a long time—not since our recovery was new. Then one day our ten-year-old daughter—in the thrall of watching a rom-com on television, no doubt dreaming of her own future proposal—asked, "Daddy, how did you propose?"

Brad and I looked at each other. The truth was he *had* said the words *will you marry me* in the pizza place. The truth was all he really remembered from that night was a warm, vague idea that someday I was the woman he wanted to marry. What he remembered more clearly was our conversation a few weeks later when I asked him to set the date, simply thinking I was closing a deal he'd already proposed.

I wished we could tell our daughter what she wanted to hear: that he'd gotten down on one knee, arranged violinists or skywriting, opened a velvet box before me. But that's not our story. Only we know that our story holds within it the best of our marriage: his unguarded love and mine in gushing return. It holds, too, our shared commitment in spite of—and later, because of—the thrill of never completely knowing one another.

As I waited for Brad to answer our daughter's question, I saw my husband just as he was when we first met: the handsome stranger. My heart raced, my pulse quickened. I wanted him even more now, years later, because of the secrets we'd shared since and the secrets left to know.

"We both sort of asked each other," he finally said.

⌒

Early in our recovery, Brad and I often rode the mountain bikes we'd gotten for our wedding. Climbing steep grades in low gears, we'd go high into the sage- and chaparral-covered hills above the Pacific Ocean. I'd watch his calves work the pedals, feeling sidesplitting pain as I toiled behind him. Still, I liked the uphill climb best—I knew I could control it. After ascending for miles, we'd rest at a crossroads where several trail systems merged and the vista stretched from ocean to valley. He'd check on me to make sure I wasn't overheated, make me take off my helmet so my brain didn't cook, cool my neck with water.

Then we'd jump back on our bikes for the descent.

Downhill was his favorite part. For this he rode behind me, urging me to go faster and faster. Our voices echoing through the canyon, sometimes I'd yell at him to stop pushing me. But invariably I laughed, giddy when the tires lost traction for just a moment and we hung midair above bumps and dips.

I used to wonder what I would have done if I'd known he was an alcoholic before we took our vows. I think back to our Making Marriage Work class and our private session with the instructor. We'd filled out individual questionnaires in preparation for the session. When we met with our teacher, he turned to Brad and said, "She's stronger than you think. She can take it." I'd waited expectantly, but my husband-to-be denied knowing what the guy was talking about. Something in the way he'd answered the questionnaire must have revealed his alcoholism. The therapist had been trying to get him to tell me.

But ignorance had truly been bliss. If I'd known before we married, I might have blown it. I might have walked away. Duped though I may have been by his secret, I became glad I hadn't known. My husband would become the first person in my life who didn't indulge my tantrums the way my mother, father, and even Wes had done. With Brad I felt foolish storming off when we fought. He dismissed drama as immature. He might never have said the exact words, but his response to my fits seemed to be "grow up." That was new.

The message I got from him was that, in fact, he would not love me unconditionally—and he didn't expect me to love him that way either. We would need to try, day by day, to be people worthy of each other's love.

I never could have known that his addiction would put us on our own paths to saving ourselves. That, at last, I would begin to grow up and find a sense of home within myself.

A
Measure
of
Desire

BRAD WAS FOUR YEARS SOBER WHEN WE MOVED TO
Maine from Los Angeles. Our daughter was nearly three, and
we had another baby on the way. Our blue Cape-style house
on three acres had the dormer windows I'd dreamed of when
I was a kid. Still early in our recovery, I imagined that a sim-
pler life in Maine would save us from further dangers that
can creep into relationships: serpents in the grass like infidelity, boredom, and debt.

That first winter, we learned to skate on frozen Megunti-
cook Lake. Around tiny islands in the middle of the lake,
Brad pushed the baby jogger that held our young daughter.
Although the ice popped like gunfire as the whole town skated
in circles, we were assured there was no danger of falling
through.

By Christmas, we placed single candles in each window
instead of stringing colored lights the way we would have
back home, and I gave birth to our son in an ice storm.

When we'd first moved to Maine, my mother had been

hurt that we'd taken her grandchildren so far from her. Then the idea struck her that she was now free to move too. She landed in New York City, managing an international law firm and living on the Upper West Side, where at last she embodied the urban sophisticate she was born to be.

"I never liked Los Angeles anyway," she said. It didn't hurt that her move put even more miles between her and my father. I would learn later that my mother's friends referred to her relocation as her own witness protection program. Nick didn't have the means to hop on a plane the way he could drive from Vegas to L.A. and ring her doorbell.

With the kids in tow, Brad and I began to regularly visit her in New York City. During one such trip, as she and I walked up Madison Avenue, I burst out with a question I'd been silently grappling with for months. "How do people go without sex?"

"They eat a lot," she joked at first, thinking I was asking rhetorically.

As we paused at the Valentino boutique window while she checked out a pair of black suede pumps, I said, "You don't."

She glanced up, catching my eye. "So by 'people' you mean me? How do I go without sex? How do you know I do?" For a moment I wondered if she had some secret lover. I dismissed the idea even though I would have been glad if she did.

"I guess because I don't see you having any."

"Well, I don't see you having any either. Does that mean you're celibate?"

Sex conversations with my mother had always made me squirm. I'd brought it up because I was growing desperate, but now I shrugged, wanting to drop the issue. She raised a perfectly arched eyebrow, assuming she knew my answer anyway. My good-looking husband and I must have sex all the time. We had the babies to prove it.

But what did she and I really know about the other's intimate life? How could she know that sobriety with all its wonders had also brought an end to the kind of closeness sex brings?

Only now do I see that it was both sobriety and parenthood that sent Brad and me retreating to separate corners after our move to Camden. Gone was the lanky kid I'd married, the lighthearted guy who had always wanted me. In his place was a quiet, broad-shouldered man with a strong jaw, focused on providing for his family. I watched him become the kind of father I'd never had, tossing our laughing children into the air, always there to catch them. Surely a good thing, yet I had trouble feeling I belonged with them. I marveled at their ease in this white-picket-fence life we were living, native speakers in a world that would always be a second language to me.

I began to wonder if I even deserved the man Brad had become. As if playing out a scene in an old movie when a doctor removes bandages from a patient's wounded eyes and everyone waits with bated breath to learn if the hero will see again—I waited for this new version of my husband to see me again and want me with the same abandon he once had. I wondered what kind of job I would get if he left me. Knowing that if he did, I would end up returning to my mother—dependent on her love once again.

The more frightened of that possibility I became, the more I began to see them: my replacements. I spotted these women the way my small son and I hunted through his *I Spy* books for "a key, a silvery fish, and a Christmas tree." Sometimes we stared and stared, unable to see the hidden objects. Other times a neon arrow might as well have pointed the way.

Surely, such an arrow directed me to the woman in the supermarket. I can see her now, even today.

It was our fourth Maine winter—not the pretty part leading up to Christmas, but the dreary aftermath. Pushing my cart past a display of scraggly poinsettias, I noticed her immediately. She was weighing snow peas, watching the scale's arrow flick near the pound mark as she tossed in handfuls. She must have felt me watching her.

"I can't get my kids to eat them," I said to explain my staring. "What's your secret?"

"A little sugar and butter."

I saw her in my kitchen then, standing at the stove in thick wool socks, sleeves pushed up. As she sautéed the peas, she reached to the cupboard for the sugar, knowing just where everything was.

Before I pushed my cart away, I thanked her. Her shell-thin nostrils drew up along with her generous smile. That was a smile Brad could love.

I forced myself to imagine her then as my children's mother, tears starting when I thought of their brown hair matching hers—my impatience, insecurity, and red hair gone from their lives, a fluke of nature corrected.

∽

I didn't tell anyone how I tortured myself choosing second-wife possibilities for my husband, how the riches shimmering in other women dazzled me. The closest I came was on a walk with my friend Annie. She was older than me with teenage daughters and a marriage I admired.

We had taken to meeting for a three-mile walk almost every day, past pine-covered hills and around the rocky edge of the ocean. Waves crashing nearby compelled nontrivial topics of conversation.

I told her that when Brad was away, I lay awake at night wondering how to escape the house if someone broke in or fire broke out. I saw myself fashioning a rope from sheets, my babies clinging to me as we climbed out the dormer windows.

I told her how my daughter was at an age when she just wanted Daddy. How one night as the four of us sat reading bedtime stories, she'd given me a little push away and told me to leave the room.

Of my daughter's rejection, my friend said, "You shouldn't leave. You are the mother." She said "mother" as if it started with a capital M—a word to be revered, a word that imparted inviolate stature. As she stopped on the path, her hand on my shoulder, she wanted me to feel the freedom of being "mother" and to, at thirty-eight years old, at last let go of the "child" mantle I'd worn so long. Rather than being the child waiting for love and approval, it was time for me to be the mother generously offering such love and understanding to her children even when they rejected her.

Days later, on another of our long walks, the idea of no longer waiting for love paved the way for another question. When I told my friend about waiting for Brad to want me again, she simply asked, "What about your desire? Don't you deserve sex?"

In the weeks that followed, I considered her question as if I'd been asked to consider a new religion. I began to toy with my desire and tease it. I noticed the tight pecs and the chin stubble on the bag boy at the grocery store. I inhaled my dashing optometrist's minty breath in the darkened exam room. I scandalized myself when—standing around at a friend's sunny backyard party, kids hooting and playing nearby, parents sipping wine—I saw our host's husband lift his arms overhead. His shirt rose as he did and my eyes traveled from the waistband of his jeans up the trail of dark hair to his navel.

That night, I claimed my yearning. In the darkness of our room, I reached for my husband. At first, the shyness between us lingered, but I did not hold back. Surprised, he kissed me with slightly opened lips. His fingers scanned my body with even more eagerness than I remembered. I wrapped my legs around him, showing how I wanted him, even though I thought a younger, nicer wife was what he deserved.

Who knew that was all it took to be happy again?

Later I would learn his reticence had never been about me. He had always relied on the balm of alcohol to face his desires, but my wanting him with such abandon changed that. I had ginned up courage for the both of us.

The next morning, I went for my usual swim at the Y.

With my goggles hanging around my neck, out of habit I chose for him the woman dressing next to me. As I busied myself with folding clothes, tucking them into my locker, I made myself jealous wondering how my blue-eyed husband would find her body—if his hands would have more desire for her.

But then I stuffed my long hair into my swim cap, my thoughts secret inside my head. With my lover's touch of the night before still humming on my skin, I turned from that woman in the locker room the same way my husband had once turned from drink.

I can't tell you the precise moment I stopped looking for my replacement to reveal herself and take away all I had ever wanted. But I know it was in Maine—before we became city people again. I know it was where we skated on a frozen lake without falling through and dove into its liquid depths when the leafy summer arrived. I know it was there that I finally realized my husband, my babies, and those dormer windows were truly mine.

Part III

Dream
Dad

THIRTY YEARS AFTER I'D FIRST SPOTTED MY FATHER ON television, I was casting the same *is-that-him* scrutiny over the arriving passengers at Reagan National Airport. Brad, the kids, and I had moved from Maine to suburban Washington, D.C., by then.

As other travelers streamed by me, I kept an eye out for Nick's signature cowboy hat. But then I caught sight of him wearing a baseball cap low and I understood he was incognito, befitting the star he was supposed to have become but never quite did.

Still, people often thought they recognized him. They'd stop him in Starbucks, pointing a finger, "Hey, aren't you . . .?" They were never sure who he was. Maybe they'd actually seen him on the old *Battlestar Galactica* or opposite a young Robert De Niro in *Bang the Drum Slowly*. Years ago, people mistook him for Nick Nolte. Now over 70, older and skinnier, they confused him with the British actor Bill Nighy. Whoever they thought he was, it didn't matter. He'd nod at them as if to say, *yes, it's me*. Satisfied, they believed he was the "someone" they wanted him to be.

It had taken Nick most of his life and mine, but he'd finally quit drinking. After he got sober he began to send me birthday cards—signed with many Xs and Os, pink and flowery with effusive definitions of wonderful daughters. He'd send me these cards even though I had never been a wonderful daughter to him. Did he know from my mother that I *could* be when I wanted to? Or was it just the kind of magical thinking he and I had always been so good at—conjuring up a story and believing it in an attempt to make it true?

When he saw me, he approached on spindly legs, his herky-jerky step the result of the accident that had led to his sobriety. Stumbling out of a bar, weaving along a dark road, he'd been unseen by the motorcyclist who mowed him down. He spent months learning to walk again. My mother was there by his side in the hospital, but I have no recollection of her telling me about the accident.

Recently, I pieced together that, as fate would have it, Nick's nearly dying happened the same year Brad got sober, and I started my own recovery. I've racked my brain trying to remember hearing about the seriousness of his condition, but I've either blocked it out or was too caught up in my own tragedies to pay attention to it. I know I never called him. I never visited.

It was he who reached out to me again. His calls started when I still lived in Maine. At first when I'd see his name on the caller ID, I'd let it ring. One day, with a decade of Al-Anon to lean on, I answered. We began talking about movies—our safe zone. We'd kept up those calls ever since. Sometimes we could talk for nearly an hour not only about movies but my kids, his dogs, my writing, the latest script he was trying to get made, and the liberal political views we shared. We avoided talking about my mother, who remained a sensitive topic.

Nick had flown in from Vegas. This trip was a twofer for him. His ultimate destination was New York City to see my mother. Once a year, she sent him a ticket because even now she couldn't escape his charms entirely. I'd finally made peace with the fact that she didn't want to.

During his New York visits, my family and I would join them in small doses—a brunch or a dinner. At eleven and eight years old, my kids didn't really know their grandfather. Even though I'd never told them to be afraid of him, on the rare occasions they'd seen Nick, they skirted him like a scary house down the block. My daughter once told me that she first heard the word "fucker" from him. She was eight. She was both startled and intrigued to know the word could expand from verb to noun.

I'd been the one to suggest he stay with us this trip. It would be a first. Before leaving for the airport, I'd made up the bed in our combination guestroom-office, placing flowers on the nightstand. He would be with us for two nights and three days.

In the airport now, I wondered if passersby registered us as father and daughter—our matching almond eyes, high cheekbones, and slim physiques a dead giveaway. As Nick and I embraced, it hit me that I'd forgotten his scent—a scent I once thought of as "handsome" and later as the smell of my own fear. Wrapping my arms around my father was like hugging one of my dogs—hard and unyielding. Our bony shoulder blades offered no comfort to one another. We'd both been beefier once, but the years had distilled us down to our essentials.

"So how ya doin' kid," he said in his soft Southern accent as he kissed the top of my head.

I scanned myself for the old hurt I'd always felt when I was with him, but it was difficult to muster. "Fine. I'm good."

He squinted one eye, as if he could see inside me to divine whether I was indeed fine. He'd been doing this since we first met, sizing me up, seeming to have some deeper wisdom about me.

Moving to baggage claim, he put a hand to my back, protectively. A flash of the time I hit him between his shoulder blades sprang to mind. I was twenty-five. "Get out of my sight," he'd screamed as he turned away to push through the swinging kitchen door of the apartment he shared with my mother. He was wearing a thin chambray shirt tucked into Lee jeans, threaded with a big western belt. My fist landed with a satisfying thwack on the soft fabric of his shirt.

After I hit him, a nervous smile twitched on my lips. As he turned back around, he stared in disbelief as I dared him to hit me back. Rather than reacting angrily, he seemed caught off guard, a wounded animal, tail between its legs.

He turned again to push through the door. "This is a daughter," I heard him say as if reminding himself, soothing himself. "This is a daughter."

All these years later, my stomach clenched now with a twinge of panic. Phone calls were easy to end, but I could not hang up on him now. In the days to come, would we circle one another the way we used to, still wild in our hearts, lunging and snarling, ready for a fight? Would he sink into one of his dark silences, unfathomable as a black hole?

I had been caught off guard before by his stony hazel eyes, jaw cocked to one side, and the gnarled knuckles on his big hands. Old images I always forgot until we were in the same room again taking up our roles: Wonderful daughter. Wolf father.

What big teeth you have.

All the better to eat you with, my dear.

Nick asked about his grandchildren as we stepped into the bright sunny afternoon. While I regaled him with their quirks and accomplishments, inside I told myself I would not be his victim again. I told myself I was different now. He was different now. Surely, the old wolf at my door could finally come inside.

I pictured my son and daughter arriving home from school in a few hours and after that, Brad would come home from work. It would be easier when I had them for backup to remind me of the woman I'd become. I knew that night we would all sit down together for dinner as if it was the most normal thing in the world to have him at our table—just a grandfather with his family.

But for now Nick and I were on our own, and I worried how we would fill the time. Then an idea struck me.

As we loaded his bags into the car, I said, "Want to go to the movies?"

He smiled. "Anything, darlin'."

At the fancy movie theater in Bethesda the early matinee was about to begin. We bought popcorn to share and bottles of water. On a Tuesday afternoon, the theater was nearly empty. Settling into the prime center section, we sank low in our velvet seats. Nick kept his hat on. The lights went down and we turned our faces toward the screen. Side by side, father and daughter, waiting for the story to unspool before us, we were full of anticipation. We were full of hope.

Ripe

WHEN I WAS TEN, MY MOTHER DECLARED ME OLD ENOUGH to stay on my own between the time school let out and the time her new Buick Skylark would roll up from work, tucking in behind our modest apartment near the Pacific Ocean. She tested me first, made me run a mock fire drill and a bad-guy-at-the-door drill. After passing her gantlet, I was liberated from my babysitter, the muumuu-wearing, horn-toenailed Mrs. Carmichael.

Although we never would have referred to me as a latch-key kid (my mother forbade me to wear a key around my neck), that's what I was. During those witching hours growing up in 1970s Los Angeles, I banded together with other untethered children. We dared each other to jump from my second-story bedroom window into thick ivy below. We roamed the neighborhood on our bikes, stole candy from the supermarket, and tried out the confessional box at St. Bernard's even though we weren't Catholic.

But sometime during sixth grade, that daring girl I'd been just the year before turned inward. Unlike my classmates, I'd begun to look more woman than girl. Boys who had once been friends accused me of stuffing my bra; they taunted and grabbed me. Too much engine under the hood for the girl I was, I didn't know how to respond. I was ashamed of their attentions mostly because my body seemed to be complicit, revealing new desires I wanted to keep secret. Only after school was out, left to my own devices and free to discover the rev and purr of my body, could I appreciate my full breasts in the mirror.

When I wasn't lost in myself, I escaped into television. This was before VCRs and TiVo. My options were soap operas, bad cartoons, game shows, and my favorite—Westerns. I liked the old ones made before I was born: *Gunsmoke*, *Wagon Train*, and *The Rifleman*. At that age, I vacillated between wanting the rifle-wielding Chuck Connors for myself and wanting him to ride up on his horse and rescue my mother.

One memorable commercial peppered these shows. Voiced by spokesman James Garner, the ad provoked a longing in me I've not forgotten, both a yearning and an urge to act. The ad was for strawberries, sponsored by the California Strawberry Growers Association.

Just as there was no on-demand television then, fruits had strict seasons that lasted only a few months. Over photos of sliced berries garnishing piping hot oatmeal and piled high on waffles laced with maple syrup, Mr. Garner teased: "Imagine strawberries on a crisp autumn or cold winter morning?" His closing pitch: "Why now? Because they're here now."

It was the *here now* that pierced me. Come October and December, I would want those strawberries, yet they would be an impossibility. The memory of May's shortcake would be my only salve.

By high school, even as the bodies of my classmates had caught up to mine, I yearned but had yet to act—to delve into real sex, to drink, to stay out late, to speak out for causes I believed in, to flout authority in any way. Not wanting to risk the judgment of others, I sat on the sidelines hungry for a taste of the grown-up things I longed to do—waiting for the day when I would finally take myself out for a spin.

 ⁓

I have a man between my thighs, but it's not what you think.

I've just swung my leg over the back of Brad's Ninja sport bike and tucked my hands into the front pockets of his leather jacket. Pulling away from the curb, already the seat vibrates my most secret places. As we take off down the block, my knees press into his hips, giving me the illusion I'm in control and steering, but with the pavement so close my life is in his hands.

The sun is neon orange and low. It's Friday evening in early September, technically still summer, the air buttery soft around me. Living on the other side of the country now in Washington, D.C., my local grocer carries strawberries year round. Not a girl anymore, I've been married to Brad for nearly twenty-five years. Our daughter is in college and our son has just started his senior year in high school.

The year before our girl went away, I was overcome with fits of crying. Like a wave I could see off in the distance from shore, our life as a family of four was coming to an end. Scared the bittersweetness of it all might pull me under, I braced myself to ride it out. That was a couple of years ago. Now with our son's departure imminent, instead of an end it feels like a beginning.

Earlier in the afternoon, I texted Brad, "How about a motorcycle ride?"

We leave our neighborhood behind, heading upcountry on roads whose names—Lost Knife, Old Gunpowder, Bowie Mill, Goshen—inspire the storyteller in me. Sitting at a stoplight, waiting for green, I glance at the people around us, car windows open, heading into their weekends. Two girls in a black SUV are laughing and singing to the radio. They beam smiles our way. Brad reaches back to pat my thigh, his hand lingering. The light changes and we're gone.

Merging into traffic, we bullet forward. I fly back a little and grip his middle tighter. *Who are we to offer up our fragile Humpty Dumpty heads like this?* I think. *A boy in his last year of high school still needs us.* I see my daughter in her twenties and remember myself at that age. *They both still need us.* Picturing friends and family, especially my mother—at seventy-three still working, still traveling the world, still beautiful—I see them at our imagined funeral, anguished and shaking their heads, saying, *Why would they be so stupid, so careless to ride like that?*

I'm not sure what Brad feels about this impending time when it will be just us again; I've been afraid to ask, and now I'm not sure I want to know. For all the time we've been together, part of me has always been on the lookout for that moment when the music will stop and harsh lights will be abruptly cast on the glow of our party.

But on this September evening, I feel freer than I have in years. As we accelerate, I don't worry about crashing and burning amidst the cars around us, even after I catch sight of a dead fawn on the shoulder, legs mangled, white belly exposed, the burnt-leaf scent of its baking carcass sharp in my nostrils. I relax, the way I learned to float as a child: lying back on the surface of the water, trusting it would hold me.

We ride for miles, as I duck down behind Brad to keep us streamlined and fast. We lean in unison as we take the curve of a freeway onramp to head for home. Shifting lanes, I instinctively turn my head as he does, looking over our shoulders in sync, as if we're part of a movie's chase scene, staying just ahead of what's after us.

Back home, we make love as we both knew we would. After all, that's what my invitation for the ride was all about. Lately, we've been having more sex than ever. Something has changed and I think it's me.

Despite having had my fair share of lovers before I married and a robust sex life with my husband, for all these years I've still been shy about revealing the magnitude of my desire. Pleasing someone else is easy for me, but enjoying my own pleasure takes a different kind of letting go. Especially without the tried-and-true de-inhibitor of alcohol. In solidarity with his sobriety, I, too, quit drinking long ago.

Yet lately, clear-eyed and sober, I flaunt my desire for him.

Walking naked into our room, no need for the cover of darkness, *Feast your eyes on me,* I'm eager to say. I am that girl in front of the mirror again, reveling in her own body, inviting my husband to be equally seduced. I've shed my youthful need to look perfect. I don't see thighs I once thought too big. Instead I appreciate slim hips and sexy shoulders. I'm grateful for the way my body makes me feel, the way it makes him feel. No longer encumbered by all the pressures and worries of raising children, now my job is to move forward, to keep living.

∽

The morning after our ride, Brad gets up early as he does every Saturday morning. While I'm still sleeping, he's opening the doors of a church basement, turning on the lights, getting the coffee ready for the AA meeting ahead. Afterwards, he calls me and laughs as he says, "I kept thinking about last night. During the Lord's Prayer I was afraid I was going to groan or say something I was thinking out loud."

After we hang up, I text him, "Come home to me. I'm not sure why, but my breasts are big and beautiful right now. We should enjoy them while we can."

I don't tell him that I know exactly why I've recently gained more than a cup size. I'd lost my ample breasts after nursing two kids, but now, in perimenopause, they are larger and firmer. Once again they are the breasts I hid from the boys in school forty years ago.

Brad and I wait for our son to head out to a friend's soccer game. As soon as he leaves, Brad comes to me, kisses my neck as he lifts my shirt.

"I wonder if kids know their parents are waiting for them

to leave the house so they can have sex," he says as we lie in bed afterwards.

"No, they're just thinking about their own escape and the sex they want to have," I say, laughing.

But even as I say this, the knowledge that next year will be different hangs over us. There will be no son down the hall, no children at home, and my full, ripe breasts may wane again for good. Gazing into my husband's eyes, I push such worries from my mind. Determined to seize this season and savor it, I run my hand along his thigh.

Glory, Glory

FOR OVER A DECADE NOW, MY MOTHER HAS LIVED IN New York City, on the ground floor of a brownstone between Riverside Drive and West End Avenue. About twice a month, I take the train from D.C.'s Union Station to see her. I navigate the bowels of Penn Station with precision born of practice, my pace calibrated with the rolling crowd as we maneuver the main fairway with its newsstands and grab-n-go lattes, salads, pizza, and gyros. Rounding one corner and then the next, I climb a short flight of stairs holding my breath against the urine-soaked landing. At last, I arrive on the subway platform, where the Uptown 1 Express will whisk me to 96th Street.

Emerging on the Upper West Side, I stop at Barzini's market for flowers—in springtime, I always hope for lilacs or peonies, my mother's favorites. The store clerk wraps them for me in a cone of thick white paper. Bouquet under my arm, I cut over from Broadway to West End. At my mother's door, digging in my bag, I fish out my set of jangling keys. Four keys to be exact: two for the outer street door, one for the vestibule door, and one that unlocks the deadbolt to my mother's apartment.

I often get there before she does. Yet my visits give her an excuse to leave earlier than usual from her windowed office high above Times Square, where she manages five floors of lawyers. Not long after I arrive, I will hear the heavy outer door pushing open, the click of her heels and the rat-a-tat-tat as she knocks, knowing I am waiting for her.

Alone in the cool of her darkened, hushed apartment, I am at home in my mother's scent—a mix of Chanel No. 5 and books. The apartment has one of those long, narrow layouts, nearly windowless except for the large sliding glass door to the garden at the back. Floor-to-ceiling, built-in mahogany shelves are overstuffed with mostly art, travel, and history titles. Treasures from her trips—jade miniatures from China; a hand-carved gazelle, lion, and zebra from Kenya; even signed and numbered Picasso and Rembrandt lithographs—perch there, mingling with the books.

The shelves line the length of the apartment's main room, which my mother has cleverly divided via furniture to signal "study," "dining room," "formal living room," and what she calls "the garden room." In winter, we spend most of our time sitting on opposite ends of the garden room's lush velvet sofa, a deep purple. But in the warmer months, we lounge in the garden or eat there—as we will tonight. Through the window, I can see the thick-trunked flowering magnolia at the center of the garden, and the red and yellow tulips my mother has planted around the edges. She doesn't really need my flower offering. Yet, it would feel graceless to come empty-handed. Once I finally became whole enough to think of her and not always of myself, giving them became a habit.

Searching the cherry wood breakfront, I find the tall crystal vase she likes. As I arrange the lilac blooms, a silent question leaves me breathless, as if a heavy boot stood on my chest: When she's gone, what will I do with all her treasures? Who will remember what she went through to get here? Who will remember her triumph?

Tonight, by the time I hear my mother's footfalls, I've got dinner almost ready. She hugs me, then can't resist turning to breathe in her lilacs, closing her eyes as she does. We carry our plates from the narrow galley kitchen into the garden to a wrought iron and glass table circled by cushioned chairs. As we continue talking, long after the sun goes down, the leavings of our dinner—steak *au poivre*, asparagus drizzled with Dijon mustard sauce, buttered baguette, and a slice of chocolate *ganache* cake to share—fade into the darkness. Fireflies begin to blink around us. We can hear neighbors on either side, but they remain unseen behind a high fence.

No doubt people up above in the neighboring buildings can look down into her garden, like something out of *Rear Window*, but the magnolia boughs shield us from view. A block away, the choir at the Greek Orthodox church on the corner is practicing. *Hallelujah! Glory, Glory,* they sing. We pause to listen. In the navy suede of the night, sitting beneath pink-bloomed branches, fallen petals all around us, no one would know we were here.

Lately, my mother has been puzzling over what she will do when she retires. Having been employed steadily since she was fourteen, she's nervous about not working. But she recently sent me an e-mail outlining the plan she will start implementing in two years: Learn Italian and take senior ballet classes now that she's quit smoking. Live in France again and in Italy for a few months. She's planning trips to India, Vietnam, Australia, and Scandinavia. But first Kenya, where we will go together this coming fall—the first trip we've taken, just the two of us, in many years. My mother is giddy at the prospect. It will be her fourth safari and my first.

As the choir continues, I sing along with the refrain: *Since I laid my burden down.* Even though I can't see my mother's face, I sense her smiling in the dark. I know I'm right when she hums *glory, glory* and I hear her soft laughter rising up into the night.

A
Different
Kind
of
Birth

I ALWAYS KNEW I WAS MY MOTHER'S MIRACLE. THE BABY
that emboldened her to leave my father, to set off on a new
life and reroute her future. But it wasn't until I was about
eleven or twelve—old enough to have my period but still my
mother's girl—that I discovered she had been a miracle baby
too. We were folding laundry. As we separated my mother's
lacy bras and panties from my days-of-the-week cotton biki-
nis, some newly stained at the crotch, we talked.

"I used to envy Grandmommy her pristine underwear,"
my mother said, speaking of her mother. Pristine because my
grandmother had had a hysterectomy a few years after my
mother was born. From twenty-eight on, she'd never had to
worry about period stains.

According to her doctor, it was a miracle my grandmother
had borne any children at all. He said this before surgically
removing any chance of her having more. But after the opera-
tion, she became sick. So sick that the hospital broke its own
rule by letting my mother—a child, and so not allowed into
such solemn places—visit her dying mother.

My grandmother, the daughter of missionaries, later said

that Jesus appeared to her when she was in the hospital. She saw him standing across a green riverbank in his long white robe, extending his hand. But she denied him. Refusing to leave her miracle baby behind, she experienced a second miracle and lived.

The births of my own children were personal marvels but, in the grand scheme, nothing extraordinary. Both were easy conceptions and healthy pregnancies. Still, birthing my son was physically the hardest thing I've ever done. He came fast, too fast for my midwife to get to the hospital. Too fast to consider an epidural, like I'd had with my daughter. Numbed that first time, I was unprepared for the heaviness between my legs, like a two-ton speculum dragging me down to some murky ocean depth as my son's head pushed its way into the world. "Open your eyes, Andrea," the doctor said, calling me back to the ocean's surface, back to that bright room and the present moment.

Like a version of the children's song "We're Going on a Bear Hunt," I knew then that I could not shut my eyes against that ocean of sensation threatening to drown me. I could not go over it. I could not go under it. I was going to have to swim through it. I've understood that ever since.

I understood it when my two-year-old daughter was attacked by our dog. Brad carried her in his arms to the ER. So much blood; a half an inch closer and her eye would have been lost.

I understood it when my son clung to my leg on the first day of kindergarten, until I pulled his little hands away and waved good-bye to him.

I understood it when my daughter was in high school and I glimpsed the hickey at the top of her breast. She turned to me and said, "Don't tell Daddy."

I understood it when the police called in the middle of the night because my son had been caught sneaking out with friends.

And I understood it when, after moving our daughter into her college dorm room, it was time to go. I'd kept it together for three days—during the cross-country flight, the trips to Target for supplies, the making of her bed, and stowing of duffle bags she'd use to come home at Christmas. Not wanting her to see me cry—oh, how I'd resented my mother's tears at my own drop-off—I turned from her after a final hug and didn't look back.

Driving to the airport, a sinkhole of grief opened within me—great, keening sobs, oddly familiar. I'd cried like this once before. When my grandmother—only fifty-nine—at last crossed over, leaving my mother and me behind. Missing her would be forever, and we would have to live through it.

No! I told myself. *How could I equate my child leaving home with death? It's just the opposite: the life force driving on, leaving behind our time together.*

And what of *my* life force?

On the other side of fifty, every month I wonder if this will be my last period, and I'm secretly relieved when it arrives again like clockwork, keeping me tethered to the self I've known so long. After I heard the news that singer Sophie Hawkins gave birth at fifty, I spent the next several days fantasizing about starting all over again.

With my history, I'm prone to believe in miracles.

Would having another baby salve my grief over my children leaving home? Or are such impulses simply vanity, wanting the world to think I'm still young enough to be making babies? Wanting to believe it myself. Forty years of period stains passed, the children of that laundry-folding girl grown and nearly gone, who am I becoming? Part of me wants to hold that woman at bay.

Yet I've learned again and again that I can't go over, under, or around, and I can't turn back. No matter how high or rough the surf, going *through* every stage is where the living is.

Each month when my period comes, I tread water in that vast ocean a little while longer, waiting for a different kind of birth.

Open your eyes, Andrea. Open your eyes.

ACKNOWLEDGMENTS

I am thankful to my many teachers, especially my Bennington MFA mentors Elizabeth Cox, Jill McCorkle, Alice Mattison, and Douglas Bauer. I am also forever grateful to Debra Spark, who encouraged me when I first returned to writing after a long hiatus, and to Bill O'Sullivan, who helped me discover creative nonfiction as my writerly home. "Thank you" does not begin to express my gratitude to my friend, guide, and first reader, Elizabeth Mosier, who helped me again and again to bring to the page the story I wanted to tell.

Thank you to the creative communities that have nurtured me along the way: Bennington MFA, The Writer's Center (Bethesda, MD), The Maine Writers & Publishers Alliance, The Martin Dibner Fellowships, Hedgebrook, and The HerStories Project. Thank you to my first editor, Bethany Root, and special thanks to Brooke Warner of She Writes Press and Crystal Patriarche of BookSparks for their inspiring vision and leadership.

Constant love and encouragement from family is a rare gift for the memoirist. I am profoundly grateful to my family for their support. Thank you to the love of my life, Brad; to my children who are a daily inspiration to be my best; to my brothers Ryan and Doug; and to the given and chosen parents I am lucky to have including Andy, Dutch, and Ruth. And thank you to my incomparable mother who has supported me in all I do always. I know reliving the events in this book is something she never wanted to do. I didn't think I could love and admire her more, but through the writing of this story I do. I also hope my readers understand that in real life, people are more complex and multifaceted than a single story will ever reveal.

The names of all those featured in this book have been changed except my husband's and mine.

◦∞◦

Versions of some chapters found previous homes in the following publications. I am so grateful to those editors who believed in my work.

"Just We Two" as "The Getaway," *Full Grown People*

"Miracle Mile," *Cleaver Magazine*

"Saviors," *Memoir Journal*

"Makeshift Twins" as "What We Don't Say," *My Other Ex: Women's Real Stories of Leaving and Losing Friendships*

"The Proposal" and "Ripe," *The Manifest-Station*

"A Measure of Desire," *The New York Times* "Modern Love" Column

"A Different Kind of Birth," *Motherwell Magazine*

book
club
discussion
guide

1. Escape is a theme in this novel. What, specifically, does the author get away from?

2. Discuss the author's relationship with her mother and the role they play in each other's lives. What is the author most grateful for about how her mother raised her? Explain the pluses and minuses of being "just we two."

3. How does the author's childhood shape her views as an adult, girlfriend, wife, and mother?

4. We see the world through the eyes of the author at different ages (child, teen, young adult, full adult looking ahead). Which events in the book resonated with you most directly and why?

5. How does the author feel meeting her father, who has become an almost mythical person to her? As she spends time with him, does she struggle with divided loyalties after a lifetime of "two-ness" with her mother?

6. What kind of man is Nick? What are his strengths and weaknesses, his flaws and contradictions?

7. What character traits does the author inherit from her parents? And how do those traits shape the author's life?

8. Discuss the theme of the denial of desires in this narrative. How do characters in this book deny their desires and what happens when they do? When should one give in to one's desires?

9. What is the most important lesson the author learns?

10. Why does the author choose to start the book with the murder of a young woman in her town?

11. How do the various locations mentioned in the book shape the author's personal journey?

12. What does the author learn about friendship and herself through her relationship with Liz?

13. What does the author learn from her relationship with Wes?

14. The author counterbalances the need to escape and the fear of being unable to get away. Have you felt that before? Or felt a similar kind of struggle between two opposites?

15. What patterns do you see in the lives of the people in this memoir? How do they compare to the patterns in your own life?

About the Author

photo credit: Eric Jensen

Andrea Jarrell's work has appeared in *The New York Times,*
The Washington Post, and many other popular and literary publications. She earned her BA in literature at Scripps College
and her MFA in creative writing and literature at Bennington
College. A Los Angeles native, she currently lives in suburban Washington, D.C.

SELECTED TITLES FROM SHE WRITES PRESS

She Writes Press is an independent publishing company
founded to serve women writers everywhere.
Visit us at www.shewritespress.com.

Fourteen: A Daughter's Memoir of Adventure, Sailing, and Survival
by Leslie Johansen Nack. $16.95, 978-1-63152-941-2. A coming-
of-age adventure story about a young girl who comes into her own
power, fights back against abuse, becomes an accomplished sailor,
and falls in love with the ocean and the natural world.

Secrets in Big Sky Country: A Memoir by Mandy Smith. $16.95,
978-1-63152-814-9. A bold and unvarnished memoir about the
shattering consequences of familial sexual abuse—and the strength
it takes to overcome them.

The Coconut Latitudes: Secrets, Storms, and Survival in the Caribbean
by Rita Gardner. $16.95, 978-1-63152-901-6. A haunting, lyrical
memoir about a dysfunctional family's experiences in a reality far
from the envisioned Eden—and the terrible cost of keeping secrets.

Veronica's Grave: A Daughter's Memoir by Barbara Bracht Donsky.
$16.95, 978-1-63152-074-7. A loss and coming-of-age story that
follows young Barbara Bracht as she struggles to comprehend the
sudden disappearance and death of her mother and cope with a
blue-collar father intent upon erasing her mother's memory.

*Letting Go into Perfect Love: Discovering the Extraordinary After
Abuse* by Gwendolyn M. Plano. $16.95, 978-1-938314-74-2. After
staying in an abusive marriage for twenty-five years, Gwen Plano
finally broke free—and started down the long road toward healing.

The Full Catastrophe: A Memoir by Karen Elizabeth Lee. $16.95,
978-1-63152-024-2. The story of a well educated, professional
woman who, after marrying the wrong kind of man—twice—finally resurrects her life.